Mike McGrath

SQL

in
easy steps

fourth edition

In easy steps is an imprint of In Easy Steps Limited
16 Hamilton Terrace · Holly Walk · Leamington Spa
Warwickshire · United Kingdom · CV32 4LY
www.ineasysteps.com

4th Edition

In Easy Steps Limited supports The Forest Stewardship Council (FSC),
the leading international forest certification organization. All our titles
that are printed on Greenpeace approved FSC certified paper carry the
FSC logo.

MIX
Paper from
responsible sources
FSC® C020837

Printed and bound in the United Kingdom

ISBN 978-1-84078-902-7

Contents

How To Use This Book

The creation of this book has provided me, Mike McGrath, a welcome opportunity to update my previous books on SQL programming with the latest techniques. All the examples I have given in this book demonstrate SQL features using the current MySQL Relational Database Management System that is supported on both Windows and Linux operating systems.

Conventions in this book

In order to clarify the code listed in the steps given in each example, I have adopted certain colorization conventions. Components of the SQL language itself are colored blue, programmer-specified names are red, numeric and string data values are black, and comments are green, like this:

```
# Insert 5 records into the "top_5_films" table.
INSERT INTO top_5_films ( position , title , year )
        VALUES ( 1 , "Citizen Kane" , 1941 ) ;
```

Additionally, in order to identify each source code file described in the steps, a colored icon and file name appears in the margin alongside the steps:

query.sql

Grabbing the source code

You can download a single ZIP archive file containing all the complete example files that appear in this book by following these easy steps:

1. Browse to **www.ineasysteps.com** then navigate to Free Resources and choose the Downloads section

2. Next, find SQL in easy steps, 4th edition in the list, then click on the hyperlink entitled All Code Examples to download the ZIP archive file

3. Now, extract the archive contents to any convenient location on your computer

I sincerely hope you enjoy discovering the powerful exciting possibilities of SQL and have as much fun with it as I did in writing this book. *Mike McGrath*

If you don't achieve the result illustrated in any example, simply compare your code to that in the original example files you have downloaded to discover where you went wrong.

1 Introducing SQL

Welcome to the exciting world of the Structured Query Language (SQL). This chapter describes how to install a free SQL database server on your system.

A programming language (pronounced either "S-Q-L" or "sequel") designed to manage database data.

What is SQL?

The Structured Query Language (SQL) is a language designed specifically for communicating with databases. Today SQL is the industry-wide standard language used by most database systems.

Databases allow collections of data to be stored in an organized manner – in the same way that data can be stored in an organized way inside files within a filing cabinet. Most modern DataBase Management Systems (DBMSs) store data in related tables, so are called Relational DBMS (RDBMS). The data stored inside databases can be examined and manipulated by SQL commands.

SQL commands are known as "queries" and utilize special keywords that can be used both to add data to a database, or extract details of data contained within a database. There are not many keywords so SQL is simple to understand but, despite its apparent simplicity, is a powerful language. Clever use of its language components enable complex sophisticated database operations to be performed.

The evolution of SQL

The model for the basis of SQL was defined back in 1970 by Dr. E. F. Codd, a researcher for IBM, in a paper entitled "A Relational Model of Data for Large Shared Data Banks". This article generated a great deal of interest in the feasibility of producing a practical commercial application of such a system.

IBM really began to develop these ideas in 1974 when they started the System/R project which eventually created the Structured English Query Language (SEQUEL). This was rewritten in 1976 to include multi-table and multi-user features and was renamed SQL in 1978. During this time other software companies had begun working on database systems based upon the SQL model. Most notable of these were Oracle, Sybase and Ingres (from the University of California's Berkeley Ingres project). The first to be released commercially was Oracle in 1979. IBM released improved database products named SQL/DS in 1982 and DB2 in 1983.

Modern versions of Oracle, Sybase, Ingres and DB2 DBMS are available today and are in widespread use around the world.

Standardization of SQL

In order to clarify the precise nature of SQL, so it could be implemented universally, each aspect of the language was defined in 1989 by the American National Standards Institute (ANSI) in a standard specification known as SQL-89. This was expanded three years later with publication of the SQL-92 specification by a joint committee of ANSI and the International Standards Organization (ISO). A third standard specification, SQL-99, was introduced in 1999 to address issues of advanced SQL syntax and has been subsequently updated with the SQL:2008 standard. Some DBMS vendors have added proprietary features to the ANSI-defined SQL standard. These extended versions even have their own names, such as PL-SQL and Transact-SQL. The examples given in this book mostly use standard ANSI-SQL so they can be applied to any DBMS.

Hot tip

"ISO" is not an acronym but is derived from the Greek word "isos" meaning equal – as in "isometric".

Forms of SQL query

There are a number of ways that SQL queries may be sent to a database to deposit or extract data:

- Directly input through an integral SQL-client application that is part of the DBMS package – this is the most straightforward method and is used in this book to demonstrate SQL features.

- Input through a third-party SQL-client application – this method communicates with the database via an intermediate software "driver". On Windows systems these are typically Open DataBase Connectivity (ODBC) data source drivers.

- From a script – often found on web servers to dynamically communicate with a database using a scripting language such as PERL, PHP or Python.

- From an Integrated Development Environment (IDE) – programmers using IDEs, such as Microsoft Visual Basic, can build programs that incorporate SQL queries to a database.

Don't forget

Learning standard ANSI-SQL enables you to interact with every major database that exists.

The next two pages outline how to execute SQL queries using a variety of popular software.

Making SQL queries

Microsoft® Access

Access is the popular database program supplied as part of the Microsoft Office suite. It is popular with Office users on stand-alone PCs and small networks. The SQL View allows you to enter SQL queries to be executed when you click the !Run button.

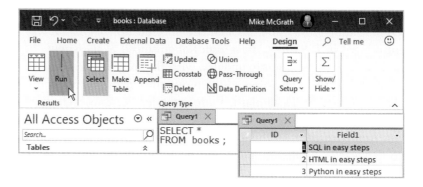

Microsoft® SQL Server

The SQL Server DBMS products from Microsoft are popular on computers running the Windows operating system. Microsoft SQL Server Express is a free, lightweight and feature-rich database for data-enabled web and Windows applications. SQL queries can be executed from the SQL Server Management Studio.

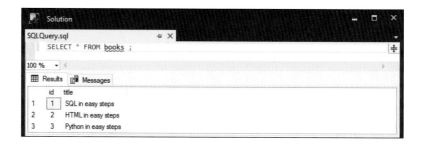

Microsoft® Visual Studio

Visual Studio can be used to create computer programs that make queries against a database via an ODBC Data Source. Simply select the Connect to Database item on the Tools menu to launch the Add Connections dialog, then choose a data source from the "Use user or system data source name" dropdown list. SQL queries can then be made from the program code.

Oracle®

The Oracle DBMS is popular and widely used in commerce. Oracle Database Express Edition (Oracle Database XE) is a free entry-level, small-footprint database that is simple to administer. SQL queries can be executed from its **SQL>** command prompt.

```
SQL Plus                                      —  □  ✕
Connected to:
Oracle Database 18c Express Edition

SQL> SELECT * FROM books;
        ID TITLE
---------- ---------------------------------------------
         1 SQL in easy steps
         2 HTML in easy steps
         3 Python in easy steps

SQL> _
```

IBM® DB2®

The DB2 DBMS is a powerful multi-platform database system. DB2-Express-C is another free full function DB2 data server. SQL queries can be executed from its **db2 =>** command prompt.

```
DB2 CLP                                       —  □  ✕
Command Line Processor for DB2 Client 11.5.0.0
db2 => SELECT * FROM books;

ID         TITLE
---------- ---------------------------------------------
         1 SQL in easy steps
         2 HTML in easy steps
         3 Python in easy steps

  3 record(s) selected.

db2 => _
```

MySQL®

The world's most popular open-source database server is the freely available MySQL DBMS product that is supplied with an integral SQL-client from which to execute SQL queries from its **mysql>** command prompt. MySQL is used throughout this book to demonstrate the SQL language. The following pages describe how to install MySQL on both Windows and Linux platforms.

Installing MySQL on Windows

The MySQL database server, which provides "back-end" storage for data-driven websites, is available for Windows, Mac OS X, and Linux operating systems as a free download.

Further guidance on installation of the MySQL Server is available at http://dev.mysql.com/ doc/refman/8.0/en/ installing.html

1 Download the MySQL Community Server installer for your system from **dev.mysql.com/downloads**

2 Run the installer and accept the License terms, then select "Server only" and click **Next** to continue

Hot tip

The MySQL Installer can be launched at any time from the Windows' Start Menu – to change the configuration or to install updates.

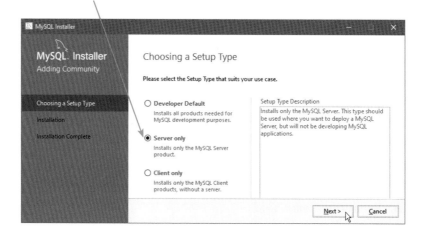

3 Click the **Execute** button to install the MySQL server

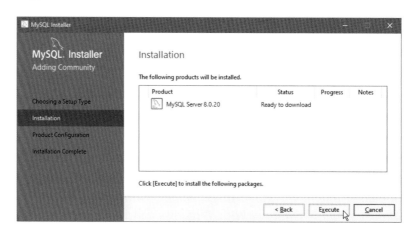

4 Click **Next**, then choose the "Standalone MySQL Server" option and click **Next** to continue

5 Select "Development Computer" as the server configuration type, then click **Next** to continue

6 Select "Use Strong Password Encryption for Authentication", then click **Next** to continue

7 Enter a root user password of your choice twice into the **Password** fields, then click **Next** to continue

Beware

By default, the MySQL Server uses port 3306. If you are running a firewall you may need to specifically allow the MySQL Server connections via this port. Refer to your firewall documentation for further guidance.

Hot tip

Write down your chosen root user password – you will need it often.

8 Click **Next** to run as a Windows Service, and **Next** to ignore Plugins, then click the **Execute** button to install the MySQL Server with your selected configuration

9 When installation completes launch the **MySQL Command Line Client** from the MySQL group that has been added to the Windows Start menu

10 Enter your password to open the MySQL monitor

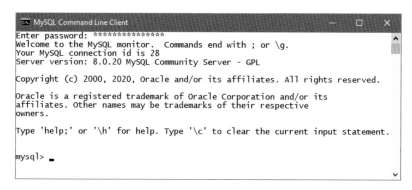

Hot tip

At the **mysql>** prompt type **exit**, **quit**, or **\q** then hit Return to close the MySQL monitor.

13

Installing MySQL on Linux

MySQL for Linux platforms can be freely downloaded from **www.mysql.com**. The recommended method of installation is to use the Redhat Package Manager (RPM), which is included with virtually all versions of Linux, or use the Package Installer that is included with the Linux Mint distro.

1 Open a web browser and visit the MySQL APT Repository at **dev.mysql.com/downloads/repo/apt**

2 Log in with an Oracle account, then download the latest MySQL configuration file

3 Next, install the file on your system

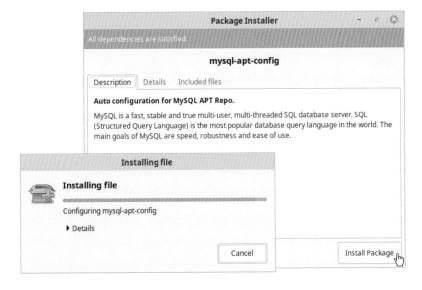

Hot tip

You can download the **mysql-apt-config** file to your Downloads folder, then double-click its file icon to open the Package Installer app.

...cont'd

4 Open a Terminal window and update the repository package lists by entering this command
sudo apt update

5 Install the MySQL server package with this command
sudo apt install mysql-server

6 When asked to confirm the installation, press the **Y** key, then hit **Enter** to continue

When the installation has completed, you should now be able to connect to the MySQL Server in a Terminal by stating the user (root), and by creating a root user password.

7 Enter this command in a Terminal window
mysql -u root -p

8 When asked, enter a root user password of your choice – you should then be welcomed to the MySQL monitor

The MySQL root user password is case-sensitive – be sure to use the correct case to connect to the MySQL server.

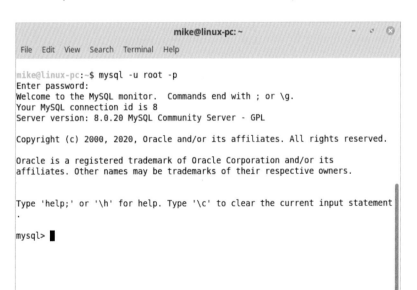

```
mike@linux-pc: ~
File  Edit  View  Search  Terminal  Help

mike@linux-pc:~$ mysql -u root -p
Enter password:
Welcome to the MySQL monitor.  Commands end with ; or \g.
Your MySQL connection id is 8
Server version: 8.0.20 MySQL Community Server - GPL

Copyright (c) 2000, 2020, Oracle and/or its affiliates. All rights reserved.

Oracle is a registered trademark of Oracle Corporation and/or its
affiliates. Other names may be trademarks of their respective owners.

Type 'help;' or '\h' for help. Type '\c' to clear the current input statement
.

mysql>
```

At the **mysql>** prompt, type **exit**, **quit**, or **\q** then hit Return to close the MySQL monitor.

Adding an ODBC connector

Usually, third-party client applications can only connect to the MySQL server if an appropriate Open DataBase Connectivity (ODBC) connector is installed on the system.

There are a whole range of ODBC connectors freely available for the MySQL server. These and other features can be added to your MySQL installation using the MySQL Installer app.

1 Launch the **MySQL Installer** app from the MySQL group on the Windows Start menu

2 Next, click the **Add** button in the Installer dialog to open a "Select Products and Features" window

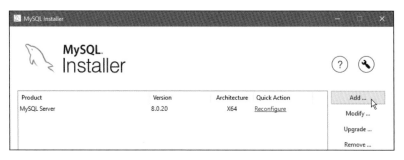

3 Expand the **MySQL Connectors** categories, then choose an ODBC connector and click the arrow button to select that connector for installation

Hot tip

Choose the connector that matches your MySQL server version (here, it's 8.0.19) and your system architecture (e.g. X64).

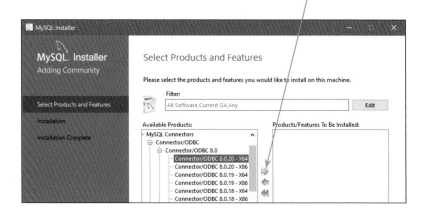

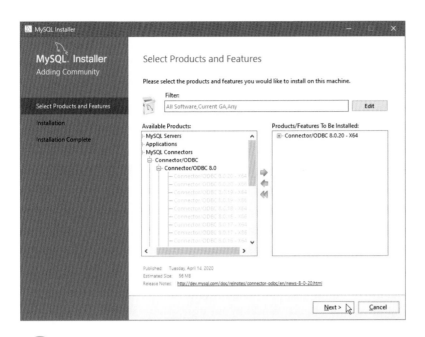

Don't forget

Your system needs to be connected to the internet to add features to your MySQL installation.

4 Click **Next** to continue, then click the **Execute** button on the next screen to install the ODBC connector

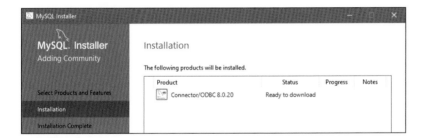

5 When installation completes, click the **Finish** button to see the connector is added to your MySQL installation

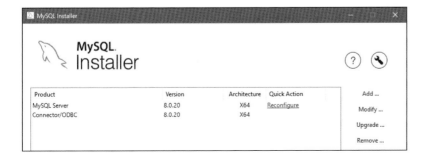

Using Microsoft Query tool

The Microsoft Query tool can be used to make SQL queries to a database. It is installed on many Windows systems without the user even knowing, because it is included with other Microsoft products such as the Excel spreadsheet program in Office.

Microsoft Query is a third-party SQL client that requires an ODBC connector to connect to the database, such as the MySQL ODBC connector installed on pages 16-17.

1 Launch the **Excel** app, then open a blank workbook

2 Select the **Data** tab on the ribbon

3 Now, click **Get Data** to open a dropdown menu of possible sources

4 Select **From Other Sources, From Microsoft Query** to open a "Choose Data Source" dialog

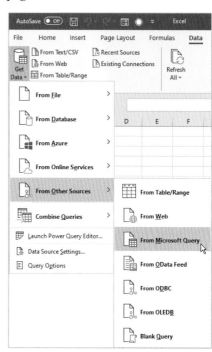

Beware

Uncheck the "Use Query Wizard to create/edit queries" option in the Choose Data Source dialog if it is checked.

5 In the "Choose Data Source" dialog, select the **MySQL Server** item, then click **OK** to see an "Add Tables" dialog appear and a disabled "Microsoft Query" window

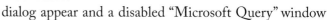

6 Close the "Add Tables" dialog to enable the "Microsoft Query" window

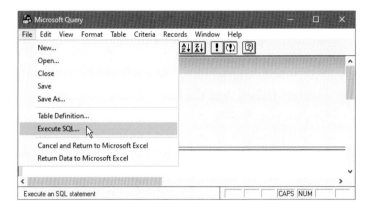

7 In the "Microsoft Query" window, click **File**, **Execute SQL...** to open an "Execute SQL" dialog

8 In the "Execute SQL" dialog type **SHOW DATABASES ;** into the "SQL statement" field

9 Click the **Execute** button to see all current MySQL databases appear listed in a "Query" dialog

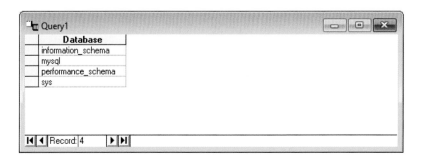

The MySQL databases shown here are those installed by default on installation – you will learn how to add your own databases in Chapter 2.

Summary

- The Structured Query Language (SQL) is the standard language for communicating with databases.

- SQL is standardized by the American National Standards Institute (ANSI) and the International Standards Organization (ISO).

- Data can be stored in a database or retrieved from a database by making an SQL query.

- Oracle Database XE, IBM DB2-Express-C and the MySQL Community Edition are all free database applications.

- SQL queries can be made from an integral client application, such as at the **mysql>** prompt in the MySQL monitor.

- Third-party applications can be used to make SQL queries via an intermediate connector using Open DataBase Connectivity (ODBC).

- Server-side scripts can make SQL queries to provide dynamic content to the user.

- Computer programs can be written to make SQL queries to a database in an Integrated Development Environment (IDE) – such as Microsoft's Visual Studio IDE.

- MySQL is the world's most popular open-source DataBase Management System (DBMS), recognized for its speed and reliability.

- There are versions of MySQL for all popular operating systems – including Windows, Linux, Solaris, and OS2.

- The Microsoft Query tool can execute SQL queries against the MySQL DBMS via an ODBC connector.

2 Getting started

This chapter demonstrates how SQL queries can reveal existing databases, create new databases, and delete existing databases.

Introducing databases

Databases are simply convenient storage containers that store data in a structured manner. Every database is composed of one or more tables that structure the data into organized rows and columns. This makes it easy to reference and manipulate the data.

Each database table column has a label to identify the data stored within the table cells in that column. Each row contains an entry called a "record" that places data in each cell along that row.

A typical simple database table looks like this:

```
+-----------+--------+---------+----------+---------------+
| member_id | fname  | lname   | tel      | email         |
+-----------+--------+---------+----------+---------------+
|         1 | John   | Smith   | 555-1234 | john@mail.com |
|         2 | Ann    | Jones   | 555-5678 | ann@mail.com  |
|         3 | Mike   | McGrath | 555-3456 | mike@mail.com |
+-----------+--------+---------+----------+---------------+
```

The rows of a database table are not automatically arranged in any particular order, so they can be sorted alphabetically, numerically or by any other criteria. It is important, therefore, to have some means to identify each record in the table. The example above allocates a "member_id" for this purpose, and this unique identifier is known as the **PRIMARY KEY**.

Storing data in a single table is very useful, but relational databases with multiple tables introduce more possibilities by allowing the stored data to be combined in a variety of ways. For instance, the following two tables could be added to the database containing the first example table shown above:

Hot tip

The column labels "member_id" and "book_id" include an underscore character because spaces are not allowed in labels.

```
+---------+-----------------+        +-----------+---------+
| book_id | title           |        | member_id | book_id |
+---------+-----------------+        +-----------+---------+
|       1 | Don Quixote     |        |         1 |       3 |
|       2 | The Great Gatsby|        |         2 |       1 |
|       3 | Moby Dick       |        |         3 |       2 |
+---------+-----------------+        +-----------+---------+
```

The table on the left lists several book titles sorted numerically by "book_id" number. The table on the right describes a relationship between the tables that links each library member to the book they have borrowed. So John (member #1) has Moby Dick (book #3), Anne (member #2) has Don Quixote (book #1), and Mike (member #3) has The Great Gatsby (book #2).

Exploring databases

The SQL query that can be used to reveal all existing databases is:

```
SHOW DATABASES ;
```

Type this query at the prompt in the MySQL Client on Windows to discover the names of all existing databases:

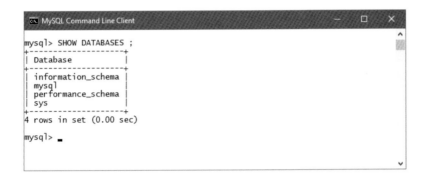

Beware

Terminate each SQL query with a semicolon in the MySQL monitor.

This MySQL installation on Windows creates four default databases named "information_schema", "mysql", "performance_schema", and "sys", which each contain data that is used by the MySQL server itself.

In Linux, start the MySQL Client in a Terminal shell window with the command **mysql -u root -p**, and enter the root user password to ensure that you have full privileges, then issue the **SHOW DATABASES** query to see all existing databases:

Don't forget

SQL keywords are not case-sensitive, but it is conventional to use uppercase characters for all SQL keywords.

Creating a database

The SQL query to create a brand new database uses the SQL keywords **CREATE DATABASE** followed by your choice of name for that database, like this:

> CREATE DATABASE *database-name* ;

So the SQL queries in the screenshots below create a new database called "library" – then confirm its existence:

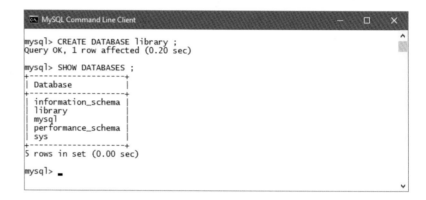

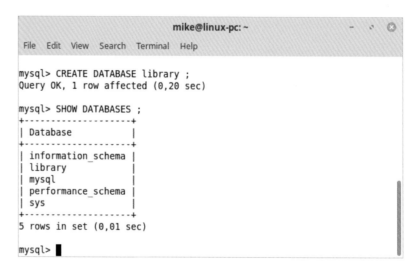

Beware

Database names may contain letters, digits, and the underscore character – but they should not contain spaces or any other characters.

If an SQL query attempts to create a new database with the name of an existing database, an error is reported. This can be avoided by qualifying the SQL query with the keywords **IF NOT EXISTS** so that it first checks to see if a database of that name already exists:

```
CREATE DATABASE IF NOT EXISTS database-name ;
```

In the screenshot below, the first SQL query attempts to create a new database called "library", which was already created in the previous example – so an error message is generated.

The second query is qualified to check that no database of that name already exists – so no error is generated.

In each case, no new database is created and the existing "library" database is unaffected by these queries:

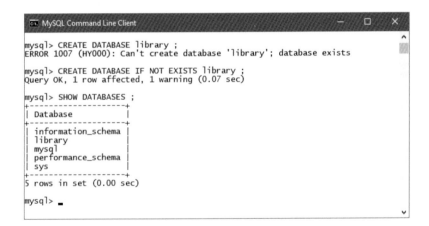

Hot tip

Use only lowercase characters for all database names to avoid any confusion of case-sensitivity.

In MySQL, database names are case-sensitive on operating systems that have case-sensitive file names, such as Linux. So MySQL on Linux regards databases "LIBRARY" and "library" as two different databases. Windows, however, makes no case-sensitive distinction, so would regard "LIBRARY" and "library" as the same database.

Deleting a database

The SQL query to delete an existing database uses the SQL keywords **DROP DATABASE** followed by its name, like this:

> DROP DATABASE *database-name* ;

The first SQL query in the screenshot below confirms the existence of a database called "library", which was created in the previous example. The subsequent queries delete the "library" database then confirm it no longer exists. Notice how multiple queries can be typed at the prompt then executed together:

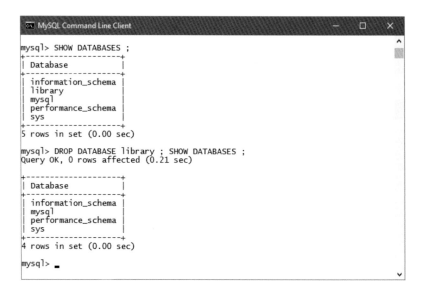

If an SQL query attempts to delete a database that does not already exist, an error is reported. This can be avoided by qualifying the SQL query with the keywords **IF EXISTS** so that it first checks to see if a database of that name already exists:

> DROP DATABASE IF EXISTS *database-name* ;

...cont'd

In the screenshot below, the SQL query first attempts to delete a database called "library", which was already deleted in the previous example – so an error message is generated.

The subsequent query is qualified to check that a database of that name already exists – so no error is generated:

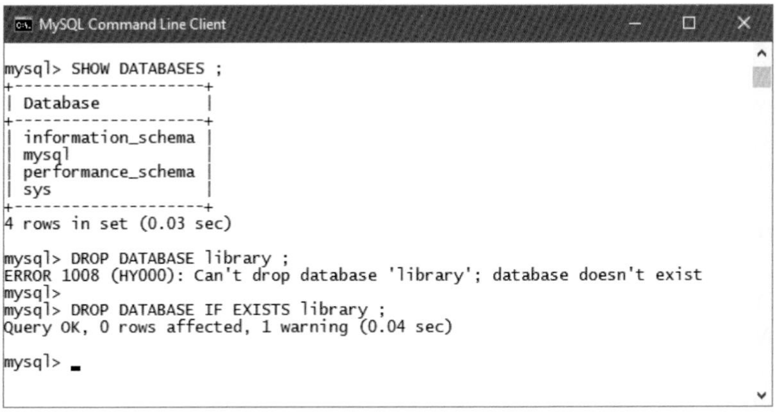

```
MySQL Command Line Client                                    —   □   ✕

mysql> SHOW DATABASES ;
+--------------------+
| Database           |
+--------------------+
| information_schema |
| mysql              |
| performance_schema |
| sys                |
+--------------------+
4 rows in set (0.03 sec)

mysql> DROP DATABASE library ;
ERROR 1008 (HY000): Can't drop database 'library'; database doesn't exist
mysql>
mysql> DROP DATABASE IF EXISTS library ;
Query OK, 0 rows affected, 1 warning (0.04 sec)

mysql> _
```

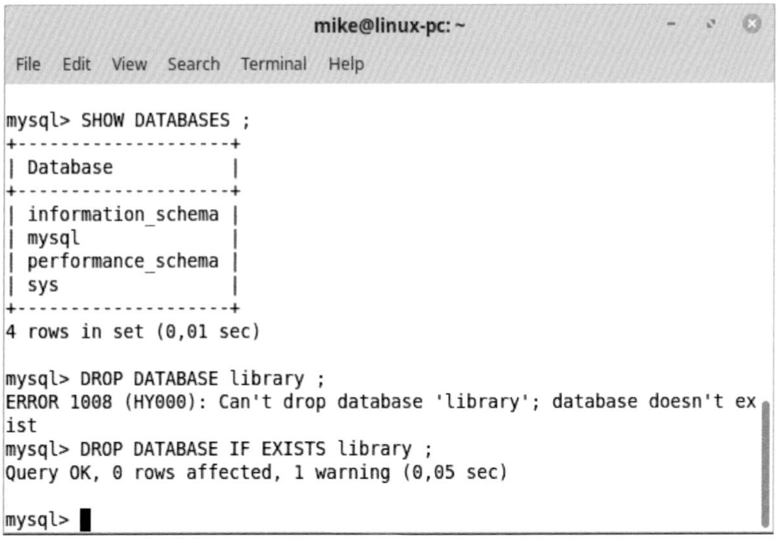

```
                    mike@linux-pc: ~              –   ·   ✕

File  Edit  View  Search  Terminal  Help

mysql> SHOW DATABASES ;
+--------------------+
| Database           |
+--------------------+
| information_schema |
| mysql              |
| performance_schema |
| sys                |
+--------------------+
4 rows in set (0,01 sec)

mysql> DROP DATABASE library ;
ERROR 1008 (HY000): Can't drop database 'library'; database doesn't ex
ist
mysql> DROP DATABASE IF EXISTS library ;
Query OK, 0 rows affected, 1 warning (0,05 sec)

mysql> ▮
```

Running SQL scripts

A number of SQL queries can be created as an SQL script that can then be run by MySQL. The script is simply a plain text file with a ".sql" file extension.

It's convenient to create a directory to store SQL scripts. The examples in the rest of this book use SQL scripts stored in a directory at **C:\SQL** on Windows systems and in a directory at **/home/user/SQL** on Linux systems.

SQL scripts are executed in the MySQL monitor by typing the word "source", followed by a space, then the full path to the script file.

Comments can usefully be added to SQL scripts to explain the purpose of particular queries. This can make scripts more comprehensible to other people or when revisiting a script at a later date. Single-line comments begin with a "#" or with "--". Multi-line C-style comments begin with "/*" and end with "*/".

The SQL script listed below reveals all databases then creates a new database if one does not already exist with that chosen name. The final query in this script confirms that the new database has indeed been created by, once more, revealing all databases:

create-db.sql

```
# Reveal existing databases.
SHOW DATABASES ;

/*
  Create a new database called "my_database" only if
  a database does not already exist with that name.
*/
CREATE DATABASE IF NOT EXISTS my_database ;

-- Reveal all databases.
SHOW DATABASES ;
```

Running the above script in the MySQL monitor executes the queries just as if they had been typed at the prompt.

The screenshots on the opposite page illustrate that the new database called "my_database" has been created on both Windows and Linux systems.

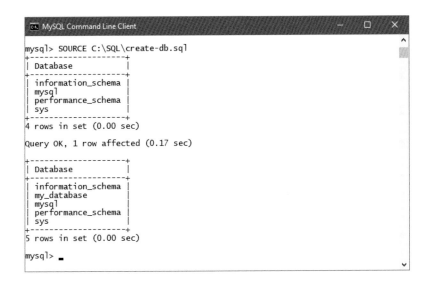

```
MySQL Command Line Client                    —   □   ×

mysql> SOURCE C:\SQL\create-db.sql
+--------------------+
| Database           |
+--------------------+
| information_schema |
| mysql              |
| performance_schema |
| sys                |
+--------------------+
4 rows in set (0.00 sec)

Query OK, 1 row affected (0.17 sec)

+--------------------+
| Database           |
+--------------------+
| information_schema |
| my_database        |
| mysql              |
| performance_schema |
| sys                |
+--------------------+
5 rows in set (0.00 sec)

mysql> _
```

The MySQL **SOURCE** keyword can alternatively be replaced by "\".

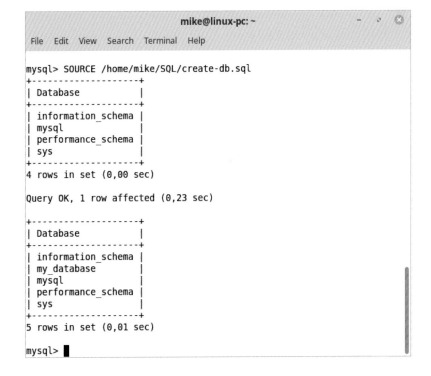

```
                 mike@linux-pc: ~              —  ⌐  ⊗

File  Edit  View  Search  Terminal  Help

mysql> SOURCE /home/mike/SQL/create-db.sql
+--------------------+
| Database           |
+--------------------+
| information_schema |
| mysql              |
| performance_schema |
| sys                |
+--------------------+
4 rows in set (0,00 sec)

Query OK, 1 row affected (0,23 sec)

+--------------------+
| Database           |
+--------------------+
| information_schema |
| my_database        |
| mysql              |
| performance_schema |
| sys                |
+--------------------+
5 rows in set (0,01 sec)

mysql> █
```

The rest of this book uses the **my_database** database created here to demonstrate features of SQL.

Summary

- Databases are containers that store data in a structured manner.

- A database table stores data in organized rows and columns.

- Each row in a database table is known as a "record".

- A **PRIMARY KEY** is a unique identifier for each record.

- Relational databases allow data stored in multiple tables to be combined in a variety of ways.

- The **SHOW DATABASES** query reveals all databases.

- Each SQL query should end with a semicolon.

- The **CREATE DATABASE** query can be used to create a new database of a specified name.

- The **CREATE DATABASE** query can be qualified with **IF NOT EXISTS** to ensure a database does not already exist of that name.

- The **DROP DATABASE** query deletes a specified database.

- The **DROP DATABASE** query can be qualified with **IF EXISTS** to ensure that a database does exist of that specified name.

- An SQL script file is a plain text file with a ".sql" file extension.

- SQL queries can be typed directly into the MySQL monitor or written in a SQL script file then run by MySQL.

- Comments can be added to an SQL script to explain the purpose of specific queries.

- Queries in an SQL script are executed by MySQL just as if they had been typed at the MySQL monitor prompt.

3 Creating database tables

This chapter demonstrates how to create a database table to store data in rows and columns, how to specify the type of data each field may store, and how to restrict field data with modifiers.

Exploring database tables

To work with any database it is necessary to first tell MySQL which database to use with this SQL query:

> USE *database-name* ;

Once the database has been selected it is possible to view a list of all the tables it contains with this SQL query:

> SHOW TABLES ;

The SQL script below contains queries to select the default "mysql" database and list all the tables it contains:

show-tbl.sql

```
# Use the default MySQL database.
USE mysql ;

# List the MySQL database tables.
SHOW TABLES ;
```

...cont'd

In order to examine any table format its column specifications can be revealed with this SQL query:

```
EXPLAIN table-name ;
```

Hot tip

This query does not reveal any data contained within the table but lists the name of each table column together with details of the type of data they may contain and any restrictions that have been placed upon them.

This example shows how table formats can be examined with the **EXPLAIN** keyword – you don't need to understand the table.

The SQL script listed below examines the table named "db" within the default "mysql" database:

```
# Use the default MySQL database.
USE mysql ;

# Examine the "db" table.
EXPLAIN db ;
```

SQL

explain-tbl.sql

```
MySQL Command Line Client                                    —    □    ×

mysql> SOURCE C:\SQL\explain-tbl.sql
Database changed
+----------------------+----------------+------+-----+---------+-------+
| Field                | Type           | Null | Key | Default | Extra |
+----------------------+----------------+------+-----+---------+-------+
| Host                 | char(255)      | NO   | PRI |         |       |
| Db                   | char(64)       | NO   | PRI |         |       |
| User                 | char(32)       | NO   | PRI |         |       |
| Select_priv          | enum('N','Y')  | NO   |     | N       |       |
| Insert_priv          | enum('N','Y')  | NO   |     | N       |       |
| Update_priv          | enum('N','Y')  | NO   |     | N       |       |
| Delete_priv          | enum('N','Y')  | NO   |     | N       |       |
| Create_priv          | enum('N','Y')  | NO   |     | N       |       |
| Drop_priv            | enum('N','Y')  | NO   |     | N       |       |
| Grant_priv           | enum('N','Y')  | NO   |     | N       |       |
| References_priv      | enum('N','Y')  | NO   |     | N       |       |
| Index_priv           | enum('N','Y')  | NO   |     | N       |       |
| Alter_priv           | enum('N','Y')  | NO   |     | N       |       |
| Create_tmp_table_priv| enum('N','Y')  | NO   |     | N       |       |
| Lock_tables_priv     | enum('N','Y')  | NO   |     | N       |       |
| Create_view_priv     | enum('N','Y')  | NO   |     | N       |       |
| Show_view_priv       | enum('N','Y')  | NO   |     | N       |       |
| Create_routine_priv  | enum('N','Y')  | NO   |     | N       |       |
| Alter_routine_priv   | enum('N','Y')  | NO   |     | N       |       |
| Execute_priv         | enum('N','Y')  | NO   |     | N       |       |
| Event_priv           | enum('N','Y')  | NO   |     | N       |       |
| Trigger_priv         | enum('N','Y')  | NO   |     | N       |       |
+----------------------+----------------+------+-----+---------+-------+
22 rows in set (0.26 sec)

mysql>
```

Creating a table

A new table can be created in a database using this query:

```
CREATE TABLE table-name ;
```

This type of query can be qualified with **IF NOT EXISTS** to ensure that a table of the specified name does not already exist:

```
CREATE TABLE IF NOT EXISTS table-name ;
```

The SQL statement in this query must be followed by parentheses defining the name of each column and the type of data that it may contain. Each column definition is separated from the next by a comma.

The SQL script listed below uses the database named "my_database" that was created in the previous chapter. It creates a table named "fruit" within that database.

The "fruit" table contains three columns named "id", "name" and "color". The **INT** SQL keyword specifies that the "id" column may only contain integer values. The **TEXT** keyword specifies that the "name" and "color" columns may only contain text values:

Hot tip

A comprehensive table of all SQL data type keywords appears on page 38.

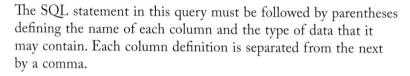

create-tbl.sql

```
# List all databases.
SHOW DATABASES ;

# Use the "my_database" database.
USE my_database ;

# Create a table called "fruit" with 3 columns.
CREATE TABLE IF NOT EXISTS fruit
(
  id        INT ,
  name      TEXT ,
  color     TEXT
) ;

# Show that the table has been created.
SHOW TABLES ;

# Confirm the "fruit" table format.
EXPLAIN fruit ;
```

Hot tip

Notice how the **CREATE TABLE** query formats the column definitions for better readability – additional spaces and line breaks are ignored.

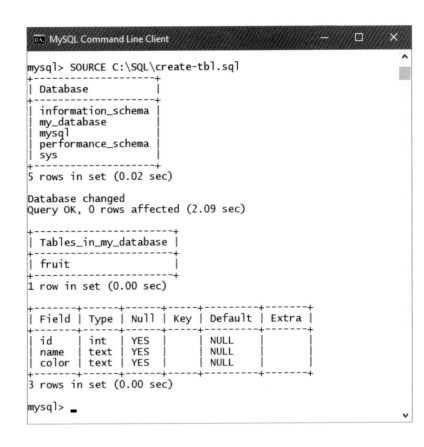

```
MySQL Command Line Client                          —   □   ×

mysql> SOURCE C:\SQL\create-tbl.sql
+--------------------+
| Database           |
+--------------------+
| information_schema |
| my_database        |
| mysql              |
| performance_schema |
| sys                |
+--------------------+
5 rows in set (0.02 sec)

Database changed
Query OK, 0 rows affected (2.09 sec)

+---------------------+
| Tables_in_my_database |
+---------------------+
| fruit               |
+---------------------+
1 row in set (0.00 sec)

+-------+------+------+-----+---------+-------+
| Field | Type | Null | Key | Default | Extra |
+-------+------+------+-----+---------+-------+
| id    | int  | YES  |     | NULL    |       |
| name  | text | YES  |     | NULL    |       |
| color | text | YES  |     | NULL    |       |
+-------+------+------+-----+---------+-------+
3 rows in set (0.00 sec)

mysql> _
```

Beware

The precise format for
database tables does vary
in other DBMSs – check
the documentation for
your version.

The **EXPLAIN** query reveals the format of the "fruit" table which
allows the "id" field to contain integers up to 11 digits long
– in actuality this is limited to values between the range of
-2147483648 to 2147483647.

In this example "YES" denotes that each field is allowed to
contain no value, defined by the **NULL** keyword. Each field has, in
fact, been created with no default value, so does contain a **NULL**
value. Note that **NULL** represents absolutely no value – this is not
the same as an empty string that is represented by "".

Deleting a table

A new table can be deleted from a database using this query:

```
DROP TABLE table-name ;
```

This type of query can be qualified with **IF EXISTS** to ensure that a table of the specified name does already exist:

```
DROP TABLE IF EXISTS table-name ;
```

When this query is executed no confirmation is sought – the table is immediately deleted along with any data that it contains.

The SQL script listed below uses the database named "my_database" that was created in the previous chapter. It creates a table named "dogs" containing two columns named "id" and "breed". After confirming that the "dogs" table has been created the script deletes that table along with the "fruit" table that was created in the previous example:

delete-tbl.sql

```
# Use the "my_database" database.
USE my_database ;

# Create a table called "dogs" with 2 columns.
CREATE TABLE IF NOT EXISTS dogs
(
  id          INT ,
  breed       TEXT
) ;

# Show that the table has been created.
SHOW TABLES ;

# Confirm the "dogs" table format.
EXPLAIN dogs ;

# Delete the "dogs" and "fruit" tables.
DROP TABLE IF EXISTS dogs ;
DROP TABLE IF EXISTS fruit ;
```

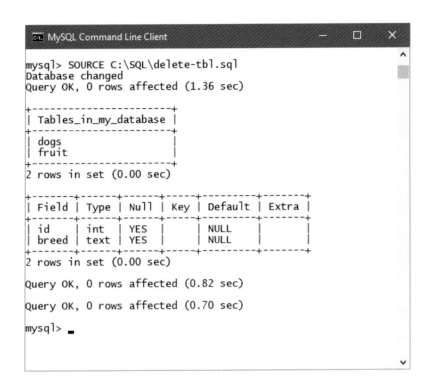

This example creates the "dogs" table in the "my_database" database alongside the existing "fruits" table. Both tables are then deleted using two **DROP TABLE** queries.

The deletion of both tables can be accomplished with a single **DROP TABLE** query by stating the table names separated by a comma.

In this case the **DROP TABLE** queries in the example code would be replaced by this single query:

```
# Delete the "dogs" and "fruit" tables.
DROP TABLE IF EXISTS dogs , fruit ;
```

Multiple tables can be deleted using this technique – but the deletion is permanent and there is no "undo" facility.

Table data types

The table below describes the range of data type specifiers that can be used to define database table columns. It is advisable to specify the permitted data type precisely. For instance, if a column only contains short strings, use **VARCHAR( )** rather than **TEXT**:

Type	Value
INT	An integer -2,147,483,648 to 2,147,483,647
DECIMAL	A floating point number that can specify the number of permissible digits. For example, DECIMAL(5,2) permits -999.99 to 999.99
DOUBLE	A long double-precision floating point number
DATE	A date in the YYY-MM-DD format
TIME	A time in the HH:MM:SS format
DATETIME	A combined date and time in the format YYY-MM-DD HH:MM:SS
YEAR	A year 1901-2155 in either YY or YYYY format
TIMESTAMP	Automatic date and time of last record entry
CHAR( )	A string of defined <u>fixed</u> length up to 255 characters long. For example, CHAR(100) pads a smaller string to make it 100 characters long
VARCHAR( )	A string of <u>variable</u> length up to 255 characters long that is stored without padding
TEXT	A string up to 65,535 characters long
BLOB	A binary type for variable data
ENUM	A single string value from a defined list. For example, ENUM("red", "green", "blue") allows entry of any one of these three colors only
SET	A string or multiple strings from a defined list. For example, SET("red", "green", "blue") allows entry of any one, or more, of these colors

The SQL script listed opposite creates a table that includes data type specifiers in the column definitions. The "id" column only accepts integer values. The date and time of each entry is automatically recorded in the "date" column. The "first_name" and "last_name" columns may each contain up to 20 characters.

Beware

The **DECIMAL** data type parameters specify the total number of permissible digits, and the number of digits that may follow the decimal point – not the number of permissible digits for the decimal point's left side, and right side.

...cont'd

```
# Use the "my_database" database.
USE my_database ;

# Create a table called "user_log" with 3 columns.
CREATE TABLE IF NOT EXISTS user_log
(
  id              INT,
  date            TIMESTAMP ,
  first_name      VARCHAR( 20 ) ,
  last_name       VARCHAR( 20 )
) ;

# Confirm the "user_log" table format.
EXPLAIN user_log ;

# Delete this sample table.
DROP TABLE user_log ;
```

data-types.sql

```
█▀ MySQL Command Line Client                    —   □   ×

mysql> SOURCE C:\SQL\data-types.sql
Database changed
Query OK, 0 rows affected (1.28 sec)

+------------+-------------+------+-----+---------+-------+
| Field      | Type        | Null | Key | Default | Extra |
+------------+-------------+------+-----+---------+-------+
| id         | int         | YES  |     | NULL    |       |
| date       | timestamp   | YES  |     | NULL    |       |
| first_name | varchar(20) | YES  |     | NULL    |       |
| last_name  | varchar(20) | YES  |     | NULL    |       |
+------------+-------------+------+-----+---------+-------+
4 rows in set (0.04 sec)

Query OK, 0 rows affected (0.54 sec)

mysql> _
```

After the **EXPLAIN** query confirms the column definitions, this sample table is deleted by a **DROP TABLE** query. Many examples in this book follow the same procedure in order to make the examples self-contained, without accumulating a large number of example tables in the "my_database" database.

Table field modifiers

In addition to specifying permissible data types, with the keywords in the table on page 38, the modifier keywords in the following table can optionally be used to further control column content:

Modifier	Purpose
NOT NULL	Insists that each record must include a data value in this column
UNIQUE	Insists that records may not duplicate any entry in this column
AUTO_INCREMENT	Available only for numeric columns, to automatically generate a number that is one more than the previous value in that column
DEFAULT	Specifies a value to be used where no value is stated for this column when a record is inserted
PRIMARY KEY	Specifies the column, or columns, to be used as the primary key for that table

Hot tip

The PRIMARY KEY modifier is described on page 42.

When it is essential that a record must include a value for a column, that column should be defined with the **NOT NULL** modifier. This allows an empty string "" to be stored there but does not allow that column to be empty or **NULL**.

When the data stored in a column should never be duplicated, that column should be defined with the **UNIQUE** modifier. For instance, to avoid the accidental duplication of product codes.

The **AUTO_INCREMENT** modifier is particularly useful to automatically generate incremental identity numbers for each row – the first row will be numbered 1, the second row 2, and so on.

Setting a column **DEFAULT** allows records to be inserted without tediously requiring a value for a column that is usually constant. For instance, a "quantity" column might usually contain a value of 1 in each record – so 1 could be set as its default value.

...cont'd

The SQL script listed below creates a table that uses modifiers in its column definitions to control the permissible content. The "id" column automatically numbers each row, and the "quantity" column will contain 1 unless another value is inserted. All the other columns must contain data values – they can't be empty or **NULL**:

```sql
# Use the "my_database" database.
USE my_database ;

# Create a table called "products" with 5 columns.
CREATE TABLE IF NOT EXISTS products
(
  id        INT           UNIQUE AUTO_INCREMENT ,
  code      INT           NOT NULL ,
  name      VARCHAR( 25 ) NOT NULL ,
  quantity  INT           DEFAULT 1 ,
  price     DECIMAL( 6,2 ) NOT NULL
) ;

# Confirm the "products" table format.
EXPLAIN products ;

# Delete this sample table.
DROP TABLE products ;
```

modifiers.sql

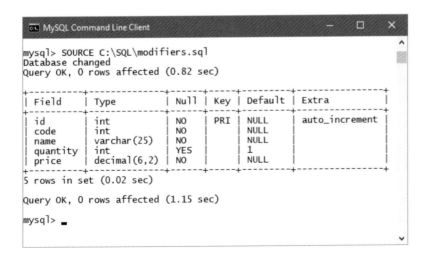

```
MySQL Command Line Client                              —  □  ✕

mysql> SOURCE C:\SQL\modifiers.sql
Database changed
Query OK, 0 rows affected (0.82 sec)

+----------+--------------+------+-----+---------+----------------+
| Field    | Type         | Null | Key | Default | Extra          |
+----------+--------------+------+-----+---------+----------------+
| id       | int          | NO   | PRI | NULL    | auto_increment |
| code     | int          | NO   |     | NULL    |                |
| name     | varchar(25)  | NO   |     | NULL    |                |
| quantity | int          | YES  |     | 1       |                |
| price    | decimal(6,2) | NO   |     | NULL    |                |
+----------+--------------+------+-----+---------+----------------+
5 rows in set (0.02 sec)

Query OK, 0 rows affected (1.15 sec)

mysql> _
```

Hot tip

The right-hand column in this illustration is headed "Extra" and notes the "auto_increment" modifier.

Setting the primary key

A **PRIMARY KEY** is a "constraint" that is applied to a column to uniquely identify each row of that database table. It ensures that the values in each row of that column are unique and never change, so those values can be used to reference any specific row.

By setting the **PRIMARY KEY** constraint it is possible to manipulate data on specific rows of the database table.

Any column can be set as the **PRIMARY KEY** but it is often the first column that is used to provide a unique identifying number.

Any column set as the **PRIMARY KEY** must meet these criteria:

- Each field in that column must have a value – it may not be empty or have a **NULL** value.

- Each value in that column must be unique – there must be no duplications.

- Each value in that column can never be modified or updated.

- Each value in that column cannot be reused – when a row is deleted, its **PRIMARY KEY** value cannot be re-assigned as the **PRIMARY KEY** value of a new row.

Notice in the previous example that MySQL automatically set the "id" column as the **PRIMARY KEY** because of the **UNIQUE** modifier that was included in that column's definition. This is indicated in the output from the **EXPLAIN** query on page 41, by the term "PRI" listed under the "Key" heading. This is logical because any column that may only contain unique values can be used to identify each table row by that column's value.

The **PRIMARY KEY** constraint can be set by adding the **PRIMARY KEY** keywords to the column definition in the **CREATE TABLE** query. Alternatively, a **PRIMARY KEY** can be set elsewhere in the **CREATE TABLE** query by stating the name of the column in parentheses after the **PRIMARY KEY** keywords.

The SQL script on the opposite page creates two tables with a **PRIMARY KEY** column set by different methods. Each table can reference any specific row by its "id" value. Notice that the **EXPLAIN** queries confirm both **PRIMARY KEY** settings.

…cont'd

```
# Use the "my_database" database.
USE my_database ;

# Create a table called "cups" with 2 columns.
CREATE TABLE IF NOT EXISTS cups
(
 id              INT      AUTO_INCREMENT PRIMARY KEY ,
 cup_pattern   VARCHAR( 25 )
) ;

# Create a table called "pots" with 2 columns.
CREATE TABLE IF NOT EXISTS pots
(
 id              INT      AUTO_INCREMENT ,
 pot_pattern   VARCHAR( 25 ) , PRIMARY KEY( id )
) ;

# Confirm the "cups" and "pots" table format.
EXPLAIN cups ; EXPLAIN pots ;

# Delete these sample tables.
DROP TABLE cups , pots ;
```

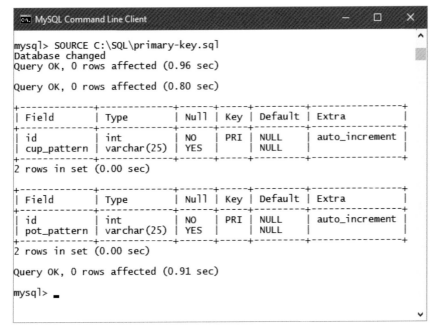

primary-key.sql

```
MySQL Command Line Client                          —    □    ×

mysql> SOURCE C:\SQL\primary-key.sql
Database changed
Query OK, 0 rows affected (0.96 sec)

Query OK, 0 rows affected (0.80 sec)

+-------------+-------------+------+-----+---------+----------------+
| Field       | Type        | Null | Key | Default | Extra          |
+-------------+-------------+------+-----+---------+----------------+
| id          | int         | NO   | PRI | NULL    | auto_increment |
| cup_pattern | varchar(25) | YES  |     | NULL    |                |
+-------------+-------------+------+-----+---------+----------------+
2 rows in set (0.00 sec)

+-------------+-------------+------+-----+---------+----------------+
| Field       | Type        | Null | Key | Default | Extra          |
+-------------+-------------+------+-----+---------+----------------+
| id          | int         | NO   | PRI | NULL    | auto_increment |
| pot_pattern | varchar(25) | YES  |     | NULL    |                |
+-------------+-------------+------+-----+---------+----------------+
2 rows in set (0.00 sec)

Query OK, 0 rows affected (0.91 sec)

mysql> _
```

Altering a table

The format of an existing database table can be changed with an **ALTER TABLE** query. This query can make a single alteration or specify a number of alterations as a comma-separated list.

An **ALTER TABLE** query can **ADD** a complete new **COLUMN** to an existing table, like this:

```
ALTER TABLE table-name
ADD COLUMN name data-type optional-modifier/s ;
```

It can also **ADD** a **PRIMARY KEY** to an existing column definition using this syntax:

```
ALTER TABLE table-name
ADD PRIMARY KEY( column-name ) ;
```

An **ALTER TABLE** query can **CHANGE** the name of an existing column. The new column will not inherit any data type or modifiers specified to the original column – these must be set anew in the **ALTER TABLE** query, like this:

```
ALTER TABLE table-name
CHANGE old-column-name new-column-name
           date-type optional-modifier/s ;
```

An **ALTER TABLE** query can also permanently delete an entire column from the table using the **DROP COLUMN** keywords:

```
ALTER TABLE table-name
DROP COLUMN column-name ;
```

The SQL script on the opposite page demonstrates all of the possibilities described on this page.

Beware

The **ALTER TABLE** query is supported by all DBMSs but there are variations in its capability – you must check the documentation for your particular DBMS to discover other **ALTER TABLE** options.

Hot tip

In the **ADD COLUMN** and **DROP COLUMN** examples, the **COLUMN** keyword is optional – it is what the manual calls "a pure noise word" that is only available to aid readability.

Beware

Care should be taken in using this technique as it will remove any data that is contained in that column – it cannot be recovered.

```sql
USE my_database ;        # Use the "my_database" database.

# Create a table called "dishes" with 3 columns.
CREATE TABLE IF NOT EXISTS dishes
(
  id          INT              NOT NULL ,
  pattern     VARCHAR( 25 )    NOT NULL ,
  price       DECIMAL( 6,2 )
) ;

EXPLAIN dishes ;         # Confirm the "dishes" table format.

# Update the "dishes" table.
ALTER TABLE dishes
  ADD PRIMARY KEY( id ) ,
  ADD COLUMN code INT UNIQUE NOT NULL ,
  CHANGE pattern dish_pattern VARCHAR( 25 ) NOT NULL ,
  DROP COLUMN price ;

EXPLAIN dishes ;         # Confirm the "dishes" table format.
DROP TABLE dishes ;      # Delete this sample table.
```

alter-tbl.sql

Altering tables that
contain data can have
unpredictable results and
should really be avoided.

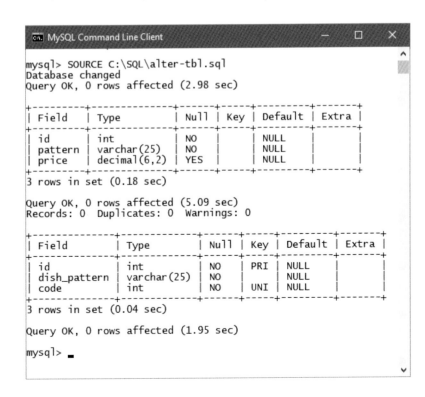

```
MySQL Command Line Client                    —    □    ×

mysql> SOURCE C:\SQL\alter-tbl.sql
Database changed
Query OK, 0 rows affected (2.98 sec)

+---------+--------------+------+-----+---------+-------+
| Field   | Type         | Null | Key | Default | Extra |
+---------+--------------+------+-----+---------+-------+
| id      | int          | NO   |     | NULL    |       |
| pattern | varchar(25)  | NO   |     | NULL    |       |
| price   | decimal(6,2) | YES  |     | NULL    |       |
+---------+--------------+------+-----+---------+-------+
3 rows in set (0.18 sec)

Query OK, 0 rows affected (5.09 sec)
Records: 0  Duplicates: 0  Warnings: 0

+--------------+-------------+------+-----+---------+-------+
| Field        | Type        | Null | Key | Default | Extra |
+--------------+-------------+------+-----+---------+-------+
| id           | int         | NO   | PRI | NULL    |       |
| dish_pattern | varchar(25) | NO   |     | NULL    |       |
| code         | int         | NO   | UNI | NULL    |       |
+--------------+-------------+------+-----+---------+-------+
3 rows in set (0.04 sec)

Query OK, 0 rows affected (1.95 sec)

mysql> _
```

Well-designed database
tables should never need
to be altered if they
anticipate all likely future
requirements.

Summary

- The **USE DATABASE** query selects a database to work with.

- The names of all the tables in a database can be revealed with the **SHOW TABLES** query.

- The format of a table can be examined with an **EXPLAIN** query.

- A new table can be created with the **CREATE TABLE** query.

- The **CREATE TABLE** query can be qualified with **IF NOT EXISTS** to ensure that a table of the specified name does not already exist.

- An existing table can be deleted with a **DROP TABLE** query.

- The **DROP TABLE** query can be qualified with **IF EXISTS** to ensure that a table of the specified name already exists.

- A column definition should specify the data type that it may contain using recognized data type keywords such as **INT, DOUBLE, DECIMAL, DATETIME, TIMESTAMP, DATE, TIME, YEAR, CHAR(), VARCHAR(), TEXT, BLOB, ENUM,** or **SET**.

- Optionally, a column definition may specify a field modifier to further control that column's permissible content to make it **NOT NULL, AUTO_INCREMENT, UNIQUE, DEFAULT,** or **PRIMARY KEY**.

- When a column is set as a **PRIMARY KEY**, each row must contain unique unalterable data in that column that can be used to identify each row of that table.

- An **ALTER TABLE** query can be used to **ADD** a new column to an existing table.

- An **ALTER TABLE** query can be used to **CHANGE** a column in an existing table.

- An **ALTER TABLE** query can be used to delete a column from an existing table with the **DROP** keyword.

- Attempting to alter tables that contain data may have unpredictable results and is not recommended.

- Well-designed database tables should never need to be altered.

4 Inserting data into tables

This chapter demonstrates how to insert complete and partial rows of data into a database table, and how to update and delete existing data within a table.

Inserting complete rows

Data can be inserted into an existing database table with an **INSERT INTO** query that first specifies the table name. The SQL **VALUES** keyword then specifies the actual data to be inserted as a comma-separated list within parentheses, like this:

INSERT INTO *table-name* VALUES (*value, value*) ;

Any text values must be enclosed within quotes.

Hot tip

In some DBMSs the **INTO** keyword may optionally be omitted – always include it in an **INSERT** query for better readability.

Each **INSERT INTO** query inserts just one row into the database table. A data value must be specified for each column – and in the corresponding order. The data to be inserted must also match the data type in each column's definition or an error will be generated. The **NULL** keyword can be specified to leave a field empty if that column's definition allows **NULL** values. All data contained in a table can be displayed with a **SELECT** query using the * wildcard and the **FROM** keyword, like this:

SELECT * FROM *table-name* ;

The following SQL script first creates a table named "prints" with three columns. Three complete rows of data are then inserted into the table by individual **INSERT INTO** queries. This is confirmed by a **SELECT** query that displays all the data within that table:

insert-data.sql

```
# Use the "my_database" database.
USE my_database ;

# Create a table named "prints" with 3 columns.
CREATE TABLE prints
(
 id          INT          NOT NULL ,
 code        VARCHAR( 8 ) NOT NULL ,
 name        VARCHAR( 20 ) NOT NULL ,
 PRIMARY KEY( id )
) ;
```

```
# Now insert 3 records into the "prints" table.
INSERT INTO prints VALUES
(
  1 , "624/1636" , "Lower Manhattan"
) ;

INSERT INTO prints VALUES
(
  2 , "624/1904" , "Hill Town"
) ;

INSERT INTO prints VALUES
(
  3 , "624/1681" , "Roscoff Trawlers"
) ;

# Show all data in the "prints" table.
SELECT * FROM prints ;

# Delete this sample table.
DROP TABLE prints ;
```

The "code" column definition allows **VARCHAR** data rather than **INT** data.

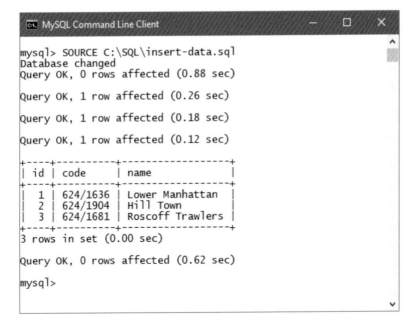

If the table columns get altered, the listed data values may not match the column definitions so an error will be generated – the example on pages 50-51 demonstrates how this can be avoided.

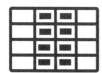

Including a columns list

The **INSERT INTO** query, introduced in the previous example on pages 48-49, can be improved by adding a "columns list" to explicitly specify the table column into which each value should be inserted. This changes the syntax of the **INSERT INTO** query to look like this:

```
INSERT INTO table-name ( column, column )
VALUES ( value, value ) ;
```

When the **INSERT INTO** query contains a columns list the DBMS matches each value to the specified column in the order in which they are listed – the value listed first will be matched to the column listed first, the value listed second will be matched to the column listed second, and so on.

The number of listed values must match the number of listed columns, but the columns need not be listed in the order in which they appear in the database table.

Additionally, a columns list need not list all the columns in the table providing that omitted columns allow **NULL** values. This allows an **INSERT INTO** query to insert only partial rows.

It is strongly recommended that all **INSERT INTO** queries should include a columns list so that the query may remain valid in the event that the table gets altered.

The SQL script on the opposite page first creates a table then inserts three records, each using a columns list.

The columns list in the first **INSERT INTO** query lists all the columns in the same order in which they appear in the table.

The columns list in the second **INSERT INTO** query again lists all the columns but in a different order to that in which they appear in the table. The values are listed in an order corresponding to this columns list.

The columns list in the third **INSERT INTO** query lists only the first two columns in the table – the value for the third column is provided by the default specified in the column definition.

Hot tip

Always include a columns list in each **INSERT INTO** query to prevent possible future database problems.

...cont'd

```
# Use the "my_database" database.
USE my_database ;

# Create a table named "towels" with 3 columns.
CREATE TABLE towels
(
  code          VARCHAR( 8 )    NOT NULL PRIMARY KEY ,
  name          VARCHAR( 20 )   NOT NULL ,
  color         VARCHAR( 20 )   DEFAULT "White"
) ;

# Insert 3 records into the "towels" table.
INSERT INTO towels ( code , name , color )
VALUES ( "821/7355" , "Dolphin" , "Blue" ) ;

INSERT INTO towels ( color , code , name )
VALUES ( "Lilac" , "830/1921" , "Daisy" ) ;

INSERT INTO towels ( code , name )
VALUES ( "830/2078" , "Starburst" ) ;

# Show all "towels" data.
SELECT * FROM towels ;
```

cols-list.sql

```
🖳 MySQL Command Line Client                    —    □    ×

mysql> SOURCE C:\SQL\cols-list.sql
Database changed
Query OK, 0 rows affected (0.79 sec)

Query OK, 1 row affected (0.13 sec)

Query OK, 1 row affected (0.14 sec)

Query OK, 1 row affected (0.23 sec)

+----------+-----------+-------+
| code     | name      | color |
+----------+-----------+-------+
| 821/7355 | Dolphin   | Blue  |
| 830/1921 | Daisy     | Lilac |
| 830/2078 | Starburst | White |
+----------+-----------+-------+
3 rows in set (0.00 sec)

mysql> _
```

The "towels" table created in this example is not deleted by this script – the table is used by other examples in this chapter.

Inserting selected data

Data can be inserted into a table from another table with an **INSERT SELECT** query using this syntax:

```
INSERT INTO destination-table ( column, column )
SELECT * FROM source-table ;
```

This example copies all the records from the "towels" table, created in the previous example on pages 50-51, into the "bath_towels" table:

insert-select.sql

```
# Use the "my_database" database.
USE my_database ;

# Create a table named "bath_towels" with 3 columns.
CREATE TABLE bath_towels
(
  code          VARCHAR( 8 )    NOT NULL PRIMARY KEY ,
  name          VARCHAR( 20 )   NOT NULL ,
  color         VARCHAR( 20 )   DEFAULT "White"
) ;

# Insert 2 records into the "bath_towels" table.
INSERT INTO bath_towels ( code , name , color )
VALUES ( "821/9735" , "Harvest" , "Beige" ) ;

INSERT INTO bath_towels ( code , name , color )
VALUES ( "821/9628" , "Wine" , "Maroon" ) ;

# Show all tables in the "my_database" database.
SHOW TABLES ;

# Show all "bath_towels" and "towels" data.
SELECT * FROM bath_towels ;
SELECT * FROM towels ;

# Add the "towels" data to the "bath_towels" table.
INSERT INTO bath_towels ( code , name , color )
SELECT * FROM towels ;

# Show all "bath_towels" data.
SELECT * FROM bath_towels ;
```

Hot tip

In this example, both tables have identically-named columns. This is not essential but the data types must match.

Hot tip

The **SELECT** query returns the value of each field on each row of the source table. These are copied, in order, into the fields of the destination table specified in the columns list.

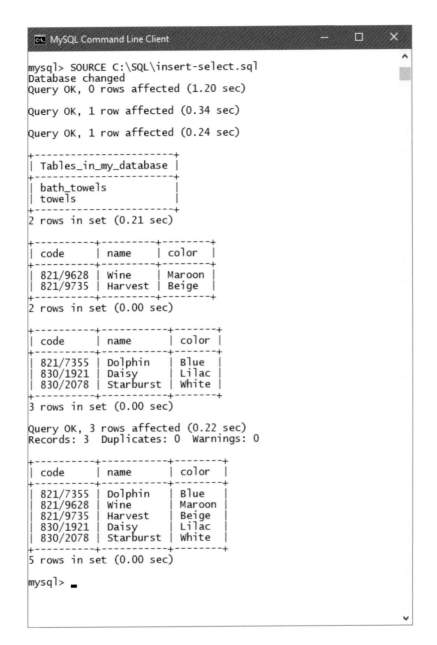

An INSERT query only inserts a single record. Multiple INSERT queries must be used to insert multiple records. An INSERT SELECT query, on the other hand, copies all the records from the source table.

Updating data

All the data contained within a column of a database table can be changed with an **UPDATE** query, which has this syntax:

```
UPDATE table-name SET column-name = value ;
```

The **UPDATE** keyword is followed by the name of the table to work with and the **SET** keyword specifies the name of the column to be updated with a new specified value.

Note that this SQL query will update every field in the specified column with the single specified value.

In the SQL script listed below, the "bath_towels" table, created in the previous example on pages 52-53, is updated so that all the fields in its "color" column are set to "White":

update-all.sql

```
# Use the "my_database" database.
USE my_database ;

# Show all "bath_towels" data.
SELECT * FROM bath_towels ;

# Update all fields in the "color" column.
UPDATE bath_towels SET color = "White" ;

# Show all "bath_towels" data.
SELECT * FROM bath_towels ;
```

The screenshot on the opposite page shows the "bath_towels" table both before and after the update has been performed as the result of executing the SQL script above.

In reality, it is not often that all the fields in a column are required to be changed to the same single value – it's more likely that only specific fields are needed to be updated.

The example on pages 56-57 shows how to identify specific column fields to be updated independently without affecting any other fields in that column.

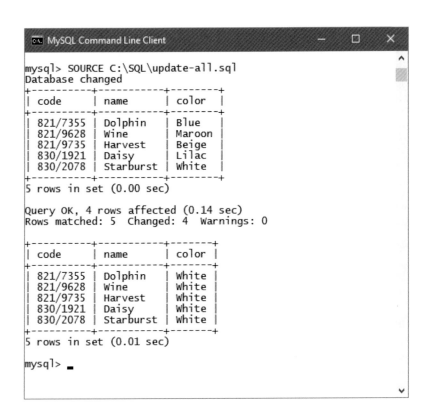

It is sometimes useful to remove all the values in a particular column using an **UPDATE** query to set each field to **NULL** – providing that the column definition allows **NULL** values.

Changing specific data

Usually, an **UPDATE** query will be required to change data contained in a particular field of a column on a specific row. The row can be identified by adding the **WHERE** keyword to the **UPDATE** query to match a value in a specified column. The syntax of the specific **UPDATE** query now looks like this:

```
UPDATE table-name SET column-name = value
WHERE column-name = value ;
```

A single **UPDATE** query can also change multiple column values on a specific row by making multiple **column = value** statements as a comma-delimited list after the **SET** keyword.

The SQL script listed below makes a number of **UPDATE** queries to the "bath_towels" table from the previous example on pages 54-55. These change the values in the "color" column. The last **UPDATE** query changes the values of the "color" column and the "name" column on the row where the "code" column has the value "821/9628":

update-where.sql

```
# Use the "my_database" database.
USE my_database ;

# Show all "bath_towels" data.
SELECT * FROM bath_towels ;

# Update specific fields in the "color" column.
UPDATE bath_towels
SET color = "Beige" WHERE name = "Harvest" ;

UPDATE bath_towels
SET color = "Blue" WHERE name = "Dolphin" ;

UPDATE bath_towels
SET color = "Lilac" WHERE name = "Daisy" ;

UPDATE bath_towels
SET name = "Tempest" , color = "Maroon"
WHERE code = "821/9628" ;

# Show all "bath_towels" data.
SELECT * FROM bath_towels ;
```

```
MySQL Command Line Client                          —    □    ✕

mysql> SOURCE C:\SQL\update-where.sql
Database changed
+----------+-----------+-------+
| code     | name      | color |
+----------+-----------+-------+
| 821/7355 | Dolphin   | White |
| 821/9628 | Wine      | White |
| 821/9735 | Harvest   | White |
| 830/1921 | Daisy     | White |
| 830/2078 | Starburst | White |
+----------+-----------+-------+
5 rows in set (0.00 sec)

Query OK, 1 row affected (0.13 sec)
Rows matched: 1  Changed: 1  Warnings: 0

Query OK, 1 row affected (0.13 sec)
Rows matched: 1  Changed: 1  Warnings: 0

Query OK, 1 row affected (0.09 sec)
Rows matched: 1  Changed: 1  Warnings: 0

Query OK, 1 row affected (0.08 sec)
Rows matched: 1  Changed: 1  Warnings: 0

+----------+-----------+-------+
| code     | name      | color  |
+----------+-----------+-------+
| 821/7355 | Dolphin   | Blue   |
| 821/9628 | Tempest   | Maroon |
| 821/9735 | Harvest   | Beige  |
| 830/1921 | Daisy     | Lilac  |
| 830/2078 | Starburst | White  |
+----------+-----------+-------+
5 rows in set (0.00 sec)

mysql> _
```

Beware

If the **WHERE** part of an **UPDATE** query is omitted, the query will update all rows – lost data cannot be recovered.

In this example, the **WHERE** keyword identifies rows by their "name" values in the first three **UPDATE** queries. This means that multiple rows could accidentally be updated if the "name" field on several rows contained identical values.

The final **UPDATE** query more correctly identifies the row by its **PRIMARY KEY** value in the "code" column – this is guaranteed to be unique, so multiple rows cannot be accidentally updated.

Don't forget

Always use the table's **PRIMARY KEY** value to identify a row.

Deleting data

Rows can be removed from a database table with a **DELETE** query. All rows can be removed with this syntax:

> DELETE FROM *table-name* ;

More usually, a specific row can be removed from a table by adding the **WHERE** keyword to a **DELETE** query to identify the row. The syntax of the **DELETE** query now looks like this:

> DELETE FROM *table-name* WHERE *column = value* ;

Two **DELETE** queries in the following SQL script first delete two specific rows of the "bath_towels" table from the previous example on pages 56-57. A further **DELETE** query removes all the other rows, then both the "bath_towels" and "towels" tables are deleted with **DROP** queries:

delete-from.sql

```
# Use the "my_database" database.
USE my_database ;

# Show all "bath_towels" data.
SELECT * FROM bath_towels ;

# Delete two specific rows.
DELETE FROM bath_towels WHERE code = "821/9735" ;
DELETE FROM bath_towels WHERE code = "821/7355" ;

# Show all "bath_towels" data.
SELECT * FROM bath_towels ;

# Delete all remaining rows in the "bath_towels" table.
DELETE FROM bath_towels ;

# Show all "bath_towels" data.
SELECT * FROM bath_towels ;

# Delete the "towels" and "bath_towels" tables.
DROP TABLE towels ;
DROP TABLE bath_towels ;

# Show tables are removed.
SHOW TABLES ;
```

```
MySQL Command Line Client                        —   □   ×

mysql> SOURCE C:\SQL\delete-from.sql
Database changed
+----------+-----------+--------+
| code     | name      | color  |
+----------+-----------+--------+
| 821/7355 | Dolphin   | Blue   |
| 821/9628 | Tempest   | Maroon |
| 821/9735 | Harvest   | Beige  |
| 830/1921 | Daisy     | Lilac  |
| 830/2078 | Starburst | White  |
+----------+-----------+--------+
5 rows in set (0.00 sec)

Query OK, 1 row affected (0.12 sec)

Query OK, 1 row affected (0.39 sec)

+----------+-----------+--------+
| code     | name      | color  |
+----------+-----------+--------+
| 821/9628 | Tempest   | Maroon |
| 830/1921 | Daisy     | Lilac  |
| 830/2078 | Starburst | White  |
+----------+-----------+--------+
3 rows in set (0.03 sec)

Query OK, 3 rows affected (0.18 sec)

Empty set (0.00 sec)

Query OK, 0 rows affected (0.69 sec)

Query OK, 0 rows affected (0.67 sec)

Empty set (0.00 sec)

mysql> _
```

Beware

If the **WHERE** part of a **DELETE** query is omitted, the query will delete all rows – the data cannot be recovered.

Notice that the **DELETE** queries in this example identify specific rows to delete by specifying their **PRIMARY KEY** "code" value after the **WHERE** keyword.

As with the previous **UPDATE** example, this is good practice – it prevents accidental deletion of data that can occur when other values are used to identify rows.

Don't forget

A **DELETE** query cannot delete the table itself – a **DROP** query is needed for that.

Summary

- Data can be inserted into a database table with an **INSERT INTO** query.

- The **VALUES** keyword is used in an **INSERT INTO** query to specify a list of data values as a comma-separated list within a single pair of parentheses.

- All text data values must be surrounded by quotes.

- The entire contents of a table can be revealed by a **SELECT * FROM** query.

- It is advisable to include a columns list in every **INSERT INTO** query to explicitly identify columns where data is to be inserted.

- Each **INSERT INTO** query inserts a single record into a table.

- A single **INSERT SELECT** query can copy all the records in a table into another table.

- All the fields in a column can be changed with an **UPDATE** query.

- The **WHERE** keyword can be added to an **UPDATE** query to identify a specific row where a field is to be changed.

- The **SET** keyword is used in an **UPDATE** query to change one or more fields in a row.

- All the rows in a table can be deleted with a **DELETE** query.

- The **WHERE** keyword can be added to a **DELETE** query to identify a specific row that is to be deleted.

- Omitting the **WHERE** part of an **UPDATE** or **DELETE** query can accidentally change or delete all table data.

- All tables should nominate a column to contain a **PRIMARY KEY**.

- The **WHERE** keyword should always identify rows by their **PRIMARY KEY** value to prevent accidental changes to table data.

5 Retrieving data from tables

This chapter demonstrates basic methods of data retrieval from database tables, and how to dynamically store retrieved data in new tables.

Retrieving a column

The SQL query to view all data in a database table was introduced in the Chapter 4. The wildcard * character, meaning "all", can be replaced with a column name to retrieve only data from that particular column. The syntax of these SQL queries look like this:

```
SELECT * FROM table-name ;
SELECT column-name FROM table-name ;
```

The following SQL script first creates and populates a table. Then, **SELECT** queries retrieve all its data and two specific columns:

select-col.sql

```
# Use the "my_database" database.
USE my_database ;

# Create a table called "microwaves".
CREATE TABLE IF NOT EXISTS microwaves
(
    id        INT            AUTO_INCREMENT PRIMARY KEY ,
    maker     VARCHAR( 20 )  NOT NULL ,
    model     VARCHAR( 20 )  NOT NULL ,
    power     INT            NOT NULL
) ;

# Insert data into the "microwaves" table.
INSERT INTO microwaves ( maker , model , power )
    VALUES ( "Sharp" , "R254SL" , 800 ) ;
INSERT INTO microwaves ( maker , model , power )
    VALUES ( "Sharp" , "R33STM" , 900 ) ;
INSERT INTO microwaves ( maker , model , power )
    VALUES ( "Sanyo" , "EMS3553" , 900 ) ;
INSERT INTO microwaves ( maker , model , power )
    VALUES ( "Panasonic" , "NNE442" , 900 ) ;
INSERT INTO microwaves ( maker , model , power )
    VALUES ( "Daewoo" , "KDR3000" , 800 ) ;

# Show all data in the "microwaves" database.
SELECT * FROM microwaves ;

# Show all data in the "maker" column.
SELECT maker FROM microwaves ;
```

...cont'd

\# Show all data in the "model" column.
SELECT model **FROM** microwaves ;

\# Delete this sample table.
DROP TABLE IF EXISTS microwaves ;

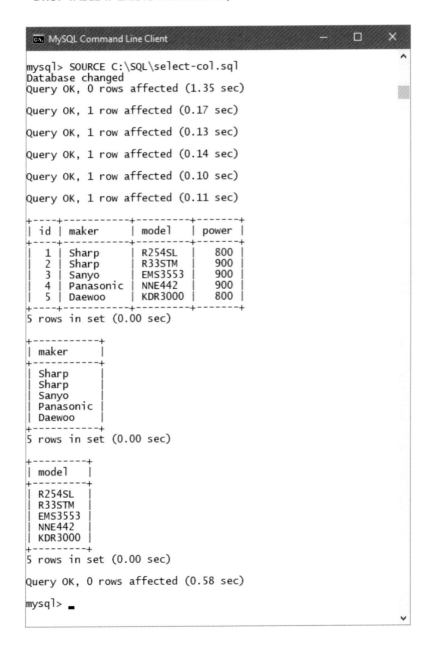

```
mysql> SOURCE C:\SQL\select-col.sql
Database changed
Query OK, 0 rows affected (1.35 sec)

Query OK, 1 row affected (0.17 sec)

Query OK, 1 row affected (0.13 sec)

Query OK, 1 row affected (0.14 sec)

Query OK, 1 row affected (0.10 sec)

Query OK, 1 row affected (0.11 sec)

+----+-----------+----------+-------+
| id | maker     | model    | power |
+----+-----------+----------+-------+
|  1 | Sharp     | R254SL   |   800 |
|  2 | Sharp     | R33STM   |   900 |
|  3 | Sanyo     | EMS3553  |   900 |
|  4 | Panasonic | NNE442   |   900 |
|  5 | Daewoo    | KDR3000  |   800 |
+----+-----------+----------+-------+
5 rows in set (0.00 sec)

+-----------+
| maker     |
+-----------+
| Sharp     |
| Sharp     |
| Sanyo     |
| Panasonic |
| Daewoo    |
+-----------+
5 rows in set (0.00 sec)

+----------+
| model    |
+----------+
| R254SL   |
| R33STM   |
| EMS3553  |
| NNE442   |
| KDR3000  |
+----------+
5 rows in set (0.00 sec)

Query OK, 0 rows affected (0.58 sec)

mysql> _
```

Don't forget

Some DBMSs may return the column values in a different order – but the result of the query is still the same.

Retrieving multiple columns

A **SELECT** query can return the data from multiple columns by including the required column names as a comma-delimited list in the query. The syntax to get multiple column data looks like this:

> SELECT *column* , *column* , *column* FROM *table-name* ;

This example builds the same table that was used in the previous example on pages 62-63, then retrieves two sets of multiple column data:

select-cols.sql

```
USE my_database ;      # Use the "my_database" database.

# Create a table called "microwaves".
CREATE TABLE IF NOT EXISTS microwaves
(
  id         INT           AUTO_INCREMENT PRIMARY KEY ,
  maker      VARCHAR( 20 ) NOT NULL ,
  model      VARCHAR( 20 ) NOT NULL ,
  power      INT           NOT NULL
) ;

# Insert data into the "microwaves" table.
INSERT INTO microwaves ( maker , model , power )
       VALUES ( "Sharp" , "R254SL" , 800 ) ;
INSERT INTO microwaves ( maker , model , power )
       VALUES ( "Sharp" , "R33STM" , 900 ) ;
INSERT INTO microwaves ( maker , model , power )
       VALUES ( "Sanyo" , "EMS3553" , 900 ) ;
INSERT INTO microwaves ( maker , model , power )
       VALUES ( "Panasonic" , "NNE442" , 900 ) ;
INSERT INTO microwaves ( maker , model , power )
       VALUES ( "Daewoo" , "KDR3000" , 800 ) ;

# Show all data in the "microwaves" database.
SELECT * FROM microwaves ;

# Show all data in the "id" and "maker" columns.
SELECT id, maker FROM microwaves ;

# Show all data in the "model" and "power" columns.
SELECT model, power FROM microwaves ;

# Delete this sample table.
DROP TABLE IF EXISTS microwaves ;
```

...cont'd

```
mysql> SOURCE C:\SQL\select-cols.sql
Database changed
Query OK, 0 rows affected (1.47 sec)

Query OK, 1 row affected (0.16 sec)

Query OK, 1 row affected (0.15 sec)

Query OK, 1 row affected (0.13 sec)

Query OK, 1 row affected (0.16 sec)

Query OK, 1 row affected (0.07 sec)

+----+-----------+---------+-------+
| id | maker     | model   | power |
+----+-----------+---------+-------+
|  1 | Sharp     | R254SL  |   800 |
|  2 | Sharp     | R33STM  |   900 |
|  3 | Sanyo     | EMS3553 |   900 |
|  4 | Panasonic | NNE442  |   900 |
|  5 | Daewoo    | KDR3000 |   800 |
+----+-----------+---------+-------+
5 rows in set (0.00 sec)

+----+-----------+
| id | maker     |
+----+-----------+
|  1 | Sharp     |
|  2 | Sharp     |
|  3 | Sanyo     |
|  4 | Panasonic |
|  5 | Daewoo    |
+----+-----------+
5 rows in set (0.00 sec)

+---------+-------+
| model   | power |
+---------+-------+
| R254SL  |   800 |
| R33STM  |   900 |
| EMS3553 |   900 |
| NNE442  |   900 |
| KDR3000 |   800 |
+---------+-------+
5 rows in set (0.00 sec)

Query OK, 0 rows affected (0.56 sec)

mysql>
```

65

Retrieving a row

A **SELECT** query can retrieve a specific row from a database table if it includes the **WHERE** keyword to identify the required row. The row should be identified by its **PRIMARY KEY** value to prevent possible duplication. The syntax of a **SELECT** query to retrieve a specific row looks like this:

```
SELECT * FROM table-name WHERE column = value ;
```

The following SQL script once again builds the table from the previous examples. An initial **SELECT** query displays all the data within that table. Then, two further **SELECT** queries display specific rows that are identified by their **PRIMARY KEY** values.

In this case, the "microwaves" table is not deleted at the end of the SQL script, so it can be used by examples later in this chapter:

select-rows.sql

```
# Use the "my_database" database.
USE my_database ;

# Create a table called "microwaves".
CREATE TABLE IF NOT EXISTS microwaves
(
    id          INT             AUTO_INCREMENT PRIMARY KEY ,
    maker       VARCHAR( 20 )   NOT NULL ,
    model       VARCHAR( 20 )   NOT NULL ,
    power       INT             NOT NULL
) ;

# Insert data into the "microwaves" table.
INSERT INTO microwaves ( maker , model , power )
        VALUES ( "Sharp" , "R254SL" , 800 ) ;
INSERT INTO microwaves ( maker , model , power )
        VALUES ( "Sharp" , "R33STM" , 900 ) ;
INSERT INTO microwaves ( maker , model , power )
        VALUES ( "Sanyo" , "EMS3553" , 900 ) ;
INSERT INTO microwaves ( maker , model , power )
        VALUES ( "Panasonic" , "NNE442" , 900 ) ;
INSERT INTO microwaves ( maker , model , power )
        VALUES ( "Daewoo" , "KDR3000" , 800 ) ;
```

...cont'd

\# Show all data in the "microwaves" database.
SELECT * FROM microwaves ;

\# Show all data in row 2.
SELECT * FROM microwaves WHERE id = 2 ;

\# Show all data in row 4.
SELECT * FROM microwaves WHERE id = 4 ;

SQL queries comprise one or more "clauses". Each clause consists of a keyword and data. For instance, **WHERE id = 3** is known as a **WHERE** clause.

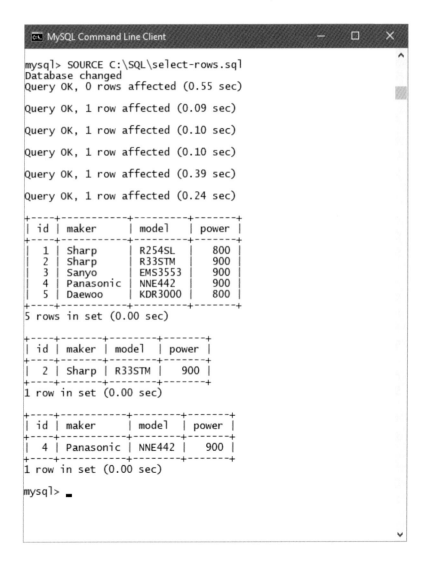

```
MySQL Command Line Client                        —    □    ✕

mysql> SOURCE C:\SQL\select-rows.sql
Database changed
Query OK, 0 rows affected (0.55 sec)

Query OK, 1 row affected (0.09 sec)

Query OK, 1 row affected (0.10 sec)

Query OK, 1 row affected (0.10 sec)

Query OK, 1 row affected (0.39 sec)

Query OK, 1 row affected (0.24 sec)

+----+-----------+---------+-------+
| id | maker     | model   | power |
+----+-----------+---------+-------+
|  1 | Sharp     | R254SL  |   800 |
|  2 | Sharp     | R33STM  |   900 |
|  3 | Sanyo     | EMS3553 |   900 |
|  4 | Panasonic | NNE442  |   900 |
|  5 | Daewoo    | KDR3000 |   800 |
+----+-----------+---------+-------+
5 rows in set (0.00 sec)

+----+-------+--------+-------+
| id | maker | model  | power |
+----+-------+--------+-------+
|  2 | Sharp | R33STM |   900 |
+----+-------+--------+-------+
1 row in set (0.00 sec)

+----+-----------+--------+-------+
| id | maker     | model  | power |
+----+-----------+--------+-------+
|  4 | Panasonic | NNE442 |   900 |
+----+-----------+--------+-------+
1 row in set (0.00 sec)

mysql> _
```

Copying retrieved data

Database tables can be created dynamically by combining a **CREATE TABLE** query with a **SELECT** query. The **SELECT** query can copy all rows, or specific rows, into the new table to populate its columns. The new table inherits the column names and features of the table from which the data is being copied.

This example dynamically creates two new tables by copying specific rows from the "microwaves" table created in the previous example on pages 66-67. It uses the values in its "power" column to select specific rows to populate each of the new tables:

copy-rows.sql

```
# Use the "my_database" database.
USE my_database ;

# Create a table called "800w_microwaves" and
# copy all 800w microwave data from "microwaves".
CREATE TABLE IF NOT EXISTS 800w_microwaves
SELECT * FROM microwaves WHERE power = 800 ;

# Create a table called "900w_microwaves" and
# copy all 900w microwave data from "microwaves".
CREATE TABLE IF NOT EXISTS 900w_microwaves
SELECT * FROM microwaves WHERE power = 900 ;

# Show all existing tables.
SHOW TABLES ;

# Show all data in the "microwaves" database.
SELECT * FROM microwaves ;

# Show all data in the "800w_microwaves" database.
SELECT * FROM 800w_microwaves ;

# Show all data in the "900w_microwaves" database.
SELECT * FROM 900w_microwaves ;

# Delete sample tables.
DROP TABLE IF EXISTS 800w_microwaves ;
DROP TABLE IF EXISTS 900w_microwaves ;

# Show all existing tables.
SHOW TABLES ;
```

```
MySQL Command Line Client                    —    □    ×

mysql> SOURCE C:\SQL\copy-rows.sql
Database changed
Query OK, 2 rows affected (1.59 sec)
Records: 2  Duplicates: 0  Warnings: 0

Query OK, 3 rows affected (1.41 sec)
Records: 3  Duplicates: 0  Warnings: 0

+----------------------+
| Tables_in_my_database |
+----------------------+
| 800w_microwaves      |
| 900w_microwaves      |
| microwaves           |
+----------------------+
3 rows in set (0.09 sec)

+----+-----------+---------+-------+
| id | maker     | model   | power |
+----+-----------+---------+-------+
|  1 | Sharp     | R254SL  |   800 |
|  2 | Sharp     | R33STM  |   900 |
|  3 | Sanyo     | EMS3553 |   900 |
|  4 | Panasonic | NNE442  |   900 |
|  5 | Daewoo    | KDR3000 |   800 |
+----+-----------+---------+-------+
5 rows in set (0.00 sec)

+----+--------+---------+-------+
| id | maker  | model   | power |
+----+--------+---------+-------+
|  1 | Sharp  | R254SL  |   800 |
|  5 | Daewoo | KDR3000 |   800 |
+----+--------+---------+-------+
2 rows in set (0.00 sec)

+----+-----------+---------+-------+
| id | maker     | model   | power |
+----+-----------+---------+-------+
|  2 | Sharp     | R33STM  |   900 |
|  3 | Sanyo     | EMS3553 |   900 |
|  4 | Panasonic | NNE442  |   900 |
+----+-----------+---------+-------+
3 rows in set (0.00 sec)

Query OK, 0 rows affected (0.73 sec)

Query OK, 0 rows affected (0.52 sec)

+----------------------+
| Tables_in_my_database |
+----------------------+
| microwaves           |
+----------------------+
1 row in set (0.01 sec)

mysql> _
```

Hot tip

Add **EXPLAIN** queries to this script to confirm that each new table inherits the column values from the original table.

Inserting selected fields

Specific fields of a table can be copied into specific fields of another table using an **INSERT INTO** query. This must state a row identifier and the column names of both the source column and the destination column. Its syntax looks like this:

```
INSERT INTO table-name ( column , column )
SELECT column , column WHERE column = value ;
```

The following SQL script first creates a table called "sharp-ovens" with two rows of data. An **INSERT INTO** query then copies two specific fields from the "microwaves" table, used in previous examples, into specific fields of the "sharp_ovens" table:

copy-fields.sql

```
# Use the "my_database" database.
USE my_database ;

# Create a table called "sharp_ovens".
CREATE TABLE sharp_ovens
(
  id       INT            AUTO_INCREMENT PRIMARY KEY ,
  model    VARCHAR( 20 )  NOT NULL ,
  power    INT            NOT NULL ,
  grill    VARCHAR( 3 )   DEFAULT "No"
) ;

# Insert data into the "sharp_ovens" table.
INSERT INTO sharp_ovens ( model , power , grill )
      VALUES ( "R654" , 800 , "Yes" ) ;
INSERT INTO sharp_ovens ( model , power , grill )
      VALUES ( "R64ST" , 800 , "Yes" ) ;

# Show all data in the "microwaves" table.
SELECT * FROM microwaves ;

# Show all data in the "sharp_ovens" table.
SELECT * FROM sharp_ovens ;

# Copy specific fields from "microwaves" to "sharp_ovens".
INSERT INTO sharp_ovens ( model , power )
SELECT model, power FROM microwaves
WHERE maker = "Sharp" ;
```

```
# Show all data in the "sharp_ovens" table.
SELECT * FROM sharp_ovens ;

# Delete sample tables used in this chapter.
DROP TABLE microwaves ;
DROP TABLE sharp_ovens ;
```

```
MySQL Command Line Client                           —    □    ×

mysql> SOURCE C:\SQL\copy-fields.sql
Database changed
Query OK, 0 rows affected (1.50 sec)

Query OK, 1 row affected (0.39 sec)

Query OK, 1 row affected (0.19 sec)

+----+-----------+----------+-------+
| id | maker     | model    | power |
+----+-----------+----------+-------+
|  1 | Sharp     | R254SL   |   800 |
|  2 | Sharp     | R33STM   |   900 |
|  3 | Sanyo     | EMS3553  |   900 |
|  4 | Panasonic | NNE442   |   900 |
|  5 | Daewoo    | KDR3000  |   800 |
+----+-----------+----------+-------+
5 rows in set (0.04 sec)

+----+--------+-------+-------+
| id | model  | power | grill |
+----+--------+-------+-------+
|  1 | R654   |   800 | Yes   |
|  2 | R64ST  |   800 | Yes   |
+----+--------+-------+-------+
2 rows in set (0.00 sec)

Query OK, 2 rows affected (0.12 sec)
Records: 2  Duplicates: 0  Warnings: 0

+----+--------+-------+-------+
| id | model  | power | grill |
+----+--------+-------+-------+
|  1 | R654   |   800 | Yes   |
|  2 | R64ST  |   800 | Yes   |
|  3 | R254SL |   800 | No    |
|  4 | R33STM |   900 | No    |
+----+--------+-------+-------+
4 rows in set (0.00 sec)

Query OK, 0 rows affected (0.60 sec)

Query OK, 0 rows affected (0.77 sec)

mysql> _
```

Summary

- The entire contents of a table can be revealed by a **SELECT * FROM** query.

- A **SELECT** query can reveal the contents of a specific column by stating the column name in place of the * wildcard character.

- Multiple column data can be retrieved by stating the column names as a comma-delimited list in a **SELECT** query.

- A specific row can be retrieved from a table by adding the **WHERE** keyword to a **SELECT** query to identify the row.

- The **CREATE TABLE** query can be combined with a **SELECT** query to dynamically create a new table populated with data from the selected existing table.

- SQL queries comprise a number of statements that are known as "clauses".

- A **WHERE** clause can be added to a combined **CREATE TABLE** and **SELECT** query to retrieve data from specific rows.

- An **INSERT INTO** query can be combined with a **SELECT** query to copy data from specific fields of one table into specific fields of another table.

- A **WHERE** clause can be added to a combined **INSERT INTO** and **SELECT** query to retrieve data from specific rows.

6

Sorting retrieved data

This chapter demonstrates how retrieved data can be sorted alphabetically or numerically in order.

Sorting a column

The data returned by a **SELECT** query may not always appear in the same order as the rows of the table – especially following updates to that table. The retrieved data can, however, be explicitly sorted into a specified order using an **ORDER BY** clause.

When the **ORDER BY** keywords are followed by a table column name, the retrieved data will be sorted into order based upon the type of data in the specified column. Typically, if the column data type is numerical, the retrieved data will be sorted in ascending numerical order. If the column data type is textual, the retrieved data will be sorted into alphabetical order from A through Z.

The SQL example script listed below demonstrates both numerical and alphabetical sorting of retrieved data:

sort-data.sql

```
# Use the "my_database" database.
USE my_database ;

# Create a table called "critters".
CREATE TABLE critters
(
  id        INT          PRIMARY KEY ,
  name      VARCHAR( 20 )  NOT NULL
) ;

# Insert 5 records into the "critters" table.
INSERT INTO critters ( id , name ) VALUES ( 3 , "Beaver" ) ;
INSERT INTO critters ( id , name ) VALUES ( 1 , "Duck" ) ;
INSERT INTO critters ( id , name ) VALUES ( 4 , "Aardvark" ) ;
INSERT INTO critters ( id , name ) VALUES ( 2 , "Elephant" ) ;
INSERT INTO critters ( id , name ) VALUES ( 5 , "Camel" ) ;

# Show all data in the "critters" table.
SELECT * FROM critters ;

# Show all data in "critters" numerically ordered.
SELECT * FROM critters ORDER BY id ;

# Show the "name" column in "critters" alphabetically.
SELECT name FROM critters ORDER BY name ;

# Delete this sample table.
DROP TABLE critters ;
```

```
MySQL Command Line Client                    —    □    ✕

mysql> SOURCE C:\SQL\sort-data.sql
Database changed
Query OK, 0 rows affected (2.76 sec)

Query OK, 1 row affected (0.35 sec)

Query OK, 1 row affected (0.44 sec)

Query OK, 1 row affected (0.29 sec)

Query OK, 1 row affected (0.28 sec)

Query OK, 1 row affected (0.29 sec)

+----+----------+
| id | name     |
+----+----------+
|  1 | Duck     |
|  2 | Elephant |
|  3 | Beaver   |
|  4 | Aardvark |
|  5 | Camel    |
+----+----------+
5 rows in set (0.00 sec)

+----+----------+
| id | name     |
+----+----------+
|  1 | Duck     |
|  2 | Elephant |
|  3 | Beaver   |
|  4 | Aardvark |
|  5 | Camel    |
+----+----------+
5 rows in set (0.00 sec)

+----------+
| name     |
+----------+
| Aardvark |
| Beaver   |
| Camel    |
| Duck     |
| Elephant |
+----------+
5 rows in set (0.00 sec)

Query OK, 0 rows affected (1.40 sec)

mysql> _
```

Beware

An **ORDER BY** clause must only appear as the final clause of a **SELECT** query – otherwise an error is generated.

Hot tip

Data retrieved from a column can be sorted by the order of another column whose data is not actually retrieved.

Sorting multiple columns

An **ORDER BY** clause can sort retrieved data by multiple columns, and the SQL script below demonstrates how this can be useful. This example sorts a number of name values into alphabetical order – firstly by last name, then by first name. Note that sorting by first name, then by last name does not produce the same result:

sort-multi.sql

```
# Use the "my_database" database.
USE my_database ;

# Create a table called "employees".
CREATE TABLE employees
(
  id            INT          AUTO_INCREMENT PRIMARY KEY ,
  first_name    VARCHAR( 20 )  NOT NULL ,
  last_name     VARCHAR( 20 )  NOT NULL
) ;

# Insert 7 records into the "employees" table.
INSERT INTO employees ( first_name , last_name )
     VALUES ( "Arthur" , "Smith" ) ;
INSERT INTO employees ( first_name , last_name )
     VALUES ( "Peter" , "Jones" ) ;
INSERT INTO employees ( first_name , last_name )
     VALUES ( "Ann" , "Smith" ) ;
INSERT INTO employees ( first_name , last_name )
     VALUES ( "Sandra" , "Williams" ) ;
INSERT INTO employees ( first_name , last_name )
     VALUES ( "Andrew" , "Smith" ) ;
INSERT INTO employees ( first_name , last_name )
     VALUES ( "Paul" , "Jones" ) ;
INSERT INTO employees ( first_name , last_name )
     VALUES ( "Sally" , "Williams" ) ;

# Show all data in the "employees" table.
SELECT * FROM employees ;

# Show both names sorted alphabetically.
SELECT first_name , last_name FROM employees
ORDER BY last_name , first_name ;

# Delete this sample table.
DROP TABLE employees ;
```

...cont'd

```
MySQL Command Line Client                    —   □   ×

mysql> SOURCE C:\SQL\sort-multi.sql
Database changed
Query OK, 0 rows affected (1.04 sec)

Query OK, 1 row affected (0.17 sec)

Query OK, 1 row affected (0.14 sec)

Query OK, 1 row affected (0.09 sec)

Query OK, 1 row affected (0.12 sec)

Query OK, 1 row affected (0.11 sec)

Query OK, 1 row affected (0.09 sec)

Query OK, 1 row affected (0.09 sec)

+----+------------+-----------+
| id | first_name | last_name |
+----+------------+-----------+
|  1 | Arthur     | Smith     |
|  2 | Peter      | Jones     |
|  3 | Ann        | Smith     |
|  4 | Sandra     | Williams  |
|  5 | Andrew     | Smith     |
|  6 | Paul       | Jones     |
|  7 | Sally      | Williams  |
+----+------------+-----------+
7 rows in set (0.00 sec)

+------------+-----------+
| first_name | last_name |
+------------+-----------+
| Paul       | Jones     |
| Peter      | Jones     |
| Andrew     | Smith     |
| Ann        | Smith     |
| Arthur     | Smith     |
| Sally      | Williams  |
| Sandra     | Williams  |
+------------+-----------+
7 rows in set (0.00 sec)

Query OK, 0 rows affected (0.50 sec)

mysql> _
```

Amend this script to **ORDER BY first_name, last_name** then compare the result to that shown in this screenshot.

Sorting by column position

The **ORDER BY** clause can optionally refer to a column of retrieved data by its position rather than its name. For instance, the first column is position 1, the next is position 2, and so on. Care must be taken to recognize that the position is that of <u>retrieved</u> columns only – not of all the columns in the table.

In the example below, the **SELECT** query returns three columns. The **ORDER BY** clause refers to the retrieved "price" column at position 3 – even though it is at position 4 in the original table:

sort-bypos.sql

```
USE my_database ;        # Use the "my_database" database.

# Create a table called "watches".
CREATE TABLE watches
(
  id          INT            AUTO_INCREMENT PRIMARY KEY ,
  model       VARCHAR( 20 )  NOT NULL ,
  style       VARCHAR( 6 )   DEFAULT "Gents" ,
  price       DECIMAL( 4,2 ) NOT NULL
) ;

# Insert 5 records into the "watches" table.
INSERT INTO watches ( model , price )
      VALUES ( "Panama" , 69.99 ) ;
INSERT INTO watches ( model , style , price )
      VALUES ( "Club" , "Ladies" , 59.99 ) ;
INSERT INTO watches ( model , price )
      VALUES ( "Avante" , 49.99 ) ;
INSERT INTO watches ( model , style , price )
      VALUES ( "Panama" , "Ladies" , 69.99 ) ;
INSERT INTO watches ( model , price )
      VALUES ( "Club" , 59.99 ) ;

# Show all data in the "watches" table.
SELECT * FROM watches ;

# Show data in "watches" ordered by style.
SELECT model , style , price FROM watches ORDER BY 2 ;

# Show data in "watches" in ascending price order.
SELECT model , style , price FROM watches ORDER BY 3 ;

DROP TABLE watches ;   # Delete this sample table.
```

Beware

This technique cannot be used when sorting by a column that is not retrieved – the **ORDER BY** clause must use the column name in that case.

```
MySQL Command Line Client                    —  □  ×

mysql> SOURCE C:\SQL\sort-bypos.sql
Database changed
Query OK, 0 rows affected (2.31 sec)

Query OK, 1 row affected (0.12 sec)

Query OK, 1 row affected (0.13 sec)

Query OK, 1 row affected (0.08 sec)

Query OK, 1 row affected (0.20 sec)

Query OK, 1 row affected (0.56 sec)

+----+--------+--------+-------+
| id | model  | style  | price |
+----+--------+--------+-------+
|  1 | Panama | Gents  | 69.99 |
|  2 | Club   | Ladies | 59.99 |
|  3 | Avante | Gents  | 49.99 |
|  4 | Panama | Ladies | 69.99 |
|  5 | Club   | Gents  | 59.99 |
+----+--------+--------+-------+
5 rows in set (0.00 sec)

+--------+--------+-------+
| model  | style  | price |
+--------+--------+-------+
| Panama | Gents  | 69.99 |
| Avante | Gents  | 49.99 |
| Club   | Gents  | 59.99 |
| Club   | Ladies | 59.99 |
| Panama | Ladies | 69.99 |
+--------+--------+-------+
5 rows in set (0.00 sec)

+--------+--------+-------+
| model  | style  | price |
+--------+--------+-------+
| Avante | Gents  | 49.99 |
| Club   | Ladies | 59.99 |
| Club   | Gents  | 59.99 |
| Panama | Gents  | 69.99 |
| Panama | Ladies | 69.99 |
+--------+--------+-------+
5 rows in set (0.00 sec)

Query OK, 0 rows affected (0.63 sec)

mysql> _
```

If the columns specified in the **SELECT** list get changed, the **ORDER BY** positions may need to be changed accordingly.

79

Although this technique means the column names need not be typed, it is easier to mistake columns – use column names rather than retrieved column positions to avoid confusion.

Setting the sort direction

By default, **SELECT** queries are automatically sorted in ascending order. An **ORDER BY** clause can explicitly specify the sort direction by adding the keywords **DESC** (descending) or **ASC** (ascending) after the name of the column to sort by.

In the SQL script listed below, the **ASC** and **DESC** keywords are used to determine the sort direction for three columns of data:

sort-dir.sql

```
# Use the "my_database" database.
USE my_database ;

# Create a table called "top_5_films".
CREATE TABLE top_5_films
(
   position      INT            PRIMARY KEY ,
   title         VARCHAR( 25 )  NOT NULL ,
   year          INT            NOT NULL
) ;

# Insert 5 records into the "top_5_films" table.
INSERT INTO top_5_films ( position , title , year )
       VALUES ( 1 , "Citizen Kane" , 1941 ) ;
INSERT INTO top_5_films ( position , title , year )
       VALUES ( 2 , "Casablanca" ,1942 ) ;
INSERT INTO top_5_films ( position , title , year )
       VALUES ( 3 , "The Godfather" , 1972 ) ;
INSERT INTO top_5_films ( position , title , year )
       VALUES ( 4 , "Gone With The Wind" , 1939 ) ;
INSERT INTO top_5_films ( position , title , year )
       VALUES ( 5 , "Lawrence Of Arabia" , 1962 ) ;

# Show all data in "top_5_films" by descending position.
SELECT * FROM top_5_films ORDER BY position DESC ;

# Show all data in "top_5_films" by ascending year.
SELECT * FROM top_5_films ORDER BY year ASC ;

# Show all data in "top_5_films" in alphabetical order.
SELECT * FROM top_5_films ORDER BY title ASC ;

# Delete this sample table.
DROP TABLE top_5_films ;
```

Hot tip

Opinions may be divided on the top five films of all time – the data in this example represents the choice of the American Film Institute.

```
■ MySQL Command Line Client                          —   □   ×

mysql> SOURCE C:\SQL\sort-dir.sql
Database changed
Query OK, 0 rows affected (0.82 sec)

Query OK, 1 row affected (0.54 sec)

Query OK, 1 row affected (0.12 sec)

Query OK, 1 row affected (0.15 sec)

Query OK, 1 row affected (0.10 sec)

Query OK, 1 row affected (0.08 sec)

+----------+--------------------+------+
| position | title              | year |
+----------+--------------------+------+
|        5 | Lawrence Of Arabia | 1962 |
|        4 | Gone With The Wind | 1939 |
|        3 | The Godfather      | 1972 |
|        2 | Casablanca         | 1942 |
|        1 | Citizen Kane       | 1941 |
+----------+--------------------+------+
5 rows in set (0.00 sec)

+----------+--------------------+------+
| position | title              | year |
+----------+--------------------+------+
|        4 | Gone With The Wind | 1939 |
|        1 | Citizen Kane       | 1941 |
|        2 | Casablanca         | 1942 |
|        5 | Lawrence Of Arabia | 1962 |
|        3 | The Godfather      | 1972 |
+----------+--------------------+------+
5 rows in set (0.00 sec)

+----------+--------------------+------+
| position | title              | year |
+----------+--------------------+------+
|        2 | Casablanca         | 1942 |
|        1 | Citizen Kane       | 1941 |
|        4 | Gone With The Wind | 1939 |
|        5 | Lawrence Of Arabia | 1962 |
|        3 | The Godfather      | 1972 |
+----------+--------------------+------+
5 rows in set (0.00 sec)

Query OK, 0 rows affected (0.71 sec)

mysql> ▄
```

Add the **DESC** keyword after each column name in the **ORDER BY** clause when sorting on multiple columns.

The default behavior when sorting treats "a" the same as "A" – but these can be treated as different values if the DBMS configuration has been modified to do so.

Summary

- The data returned by a **SELECT** query may not appear in the same order as it does in the database table.

- An **ORDER BY** clause can be added to a **SELECT** query to explicitly specify how the retrieved data should be ordered.

- The **ORDER BY** keywords specify a column upon which to order the retrieved data.

- If the column specified to sort by contains a textual data type, the retrieved data will, by default, be sorted alphabetically A-Z.

- If the column specified to sort by contains numerical data, the retrieved data will, by default, be sorted numerically in ascending order. For instance, 1-1000.

- An **ORDER BY** clause can only appear as the final clause in a **SELECT** query.

- An **ORDER BY** clause can specify multiple columns to sort by. This is particularly useful to sort names into alphabetical order by both first name and last name.

- The column to sort by in an **ORDER BY** clause can alternatively be referred to by its ordinal position in the retrieved data.

- When referencing the column to sort by using its position, any changes to columns in the **SELECT** list may need to be reflected in changes to the **ORDER BY** clause.

- The sort direction can be explicitly specified by adding either **ASC** or **DESC** in the **ORDER BY** clause.

7 Simple data filtering

This chapter demonstrates how SELECT queries can retrieve specific data by stating a test using various comparison operators.

Making comparisons

The database tables in the examples in this book only contain a few records because of space limitations – in reality, database tables usually contain many records.

Queries against large database tables generally seek a subset of the table's data rather than its entire contents. This is achieved by stating a "search criteria" in the SQL query.

In a **SELECT** query, the search criteria can be specified in its **WHERE** clause, using a comparison operator to test whether a condition is met in any particular record. When the condition is met, the query will return the data in that record – when the test fails, no data will be returned.

Each comparison is an evaluation that is "true" when the test succeeds, and "false" when the test fails.

The equality comparison operator, represented by the = character, was introduced in the example on page 66. This compares a database table's field value with a specified test value, then returns data from that record only when the comparison is true. When the comparison is false, no data is returned by the query.

Making comparative tests in this way allows the data returned by an SQL query to be selectively filtered according to the requirements of the query.

It is, of course, also possible to make an SQL query to retrieve all the data in a table from an application that subsequently filters the data according to requirements. For instance, a C++ client application could query a database to return all its records then loop through each record selecting specific data according to given search criteria.

This is, however, a slower and less efficient technique – all DBMS software is optimized to provide fast and accurate filtration of data stored within database tables. It is recommended that it should always be the SQL query that filters the data rather than the application making the query.

In addition to the equality operator introduced earlier, there are a number of other comparison operators that can be used in a **WHERE** clause to specify search criteria.

The comparison operators vary from one DBMS to another, but the most commonly recognized comparison operators are listed in the table below:

Hot tip

Check the documentation for your DBMS to discover if these and other comparison operators are supported.

Operator	Description
=	Equality
!=	Inequality
<	Less than
<=	Less than or equal
>	More than
>=	More than or equal
BETWEEN min **AND** max	Within the range min to max
IS NULL	Is a NULL value
IS NOT NULL	Is not a NULL value

A frequently-found alternative to the != inequality operator is the <> inequality operator. This book uses the != version because that also appears in other languages, such as JavaScript.

Examples that follow in the rest of this chapter demonstrate how each of the comparison operators can be used to select specific data from a database table.

Comparing a single value

The most simple comparison in a **SELECT** query's **WHERE** clause just compares a specified field on each row against a given value. When the comparison is true, the data is retrieved from that row – otherwise that row is ignored.

The following SQL script demonstrates the comparison of the value contained in each row of a table column named "price" against a specified value. In this case, all the data from a row where the comparison is true is retrieved by the **SELECT** query. The data returned by the queries in this example illustrates the difference between the < "less than" operator, the > "greater than" operator, and the <= "less than or equal to" operator:

filter-one.sql

```
# Use the "my_database" database.
USE my_database ;

# Create a table called "clock radios".
CREATE TABLE IF NOT EXISTS clock_radios
(
   code          CHAR( 8 )          PRIMARY KEY ,
   make          VARCHAR( 25 )     NOT NULL ,
   model         VARCHAR( 25 )     NOT NULL ,
   price         DECIMAL( 4,2 )    NOT NULL
) ;

# Insert 5 records into the "clock_radios" table.
INSERT INTO clock_radios ( code , make , model , price )
  VALUES ( "512/4792"  "Alba"  "C2108"  6.75 ) ;
INSERT INTO clock_radios ( code , make , model , price )
  VALUES ( "512/4125"  "Hitachi"  "KC30"  8.99 ) ;
INSERT INTO clock_radios ( code , make , model , price )
  VALUES ( "512/1458"  "Philips"  "AJ3010"  19.99 ) ;
INSERT INTO clock_radios ( code , make , model , price )
  VALUES ( "512/3669"  "Morphy Richards"  "28025"  19.99 ) ;
INSERT INTO clock_radios ( code , make , model , price )
  VALUES ( "512/1444"  "Sony"  "C253"  29.49 ) ;

# Show records in "clock_radios" if price is below 19.99.
SELECT * FROM clock_radios WHERE price < 19.99 ;

# Show records in "clock_radios" if price is above 19.99.
SELECT * FROM clock_radios WHERE price > 19.99 ;
```

Show records if price is either 19.99 or less.
SELECT * FROM clock_radios **WHERE** price <= **19.99** ;

Delete this sample table.
DROP TABLE IF EXISTS clock_radios ;

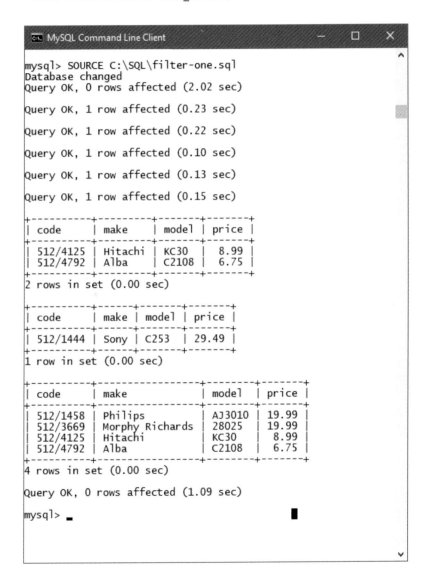

Values that are text "strings" must be surrounded by quotes.

Comparing a range of values

The **WHERE** clause in a **SELECT** query can test if the value in a column field falls within a specified range using the SQL keywords **BETWEEN** and **AND**. The syntax for such a query looks like this:

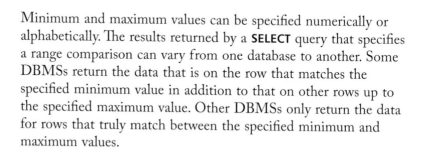

```
SELECT data FROM table-name
WHERE column BETWEEN min AND max ;
```

Minimum and maximum values can be specified numerically or alphabetically. The results returned by a **SELECT** query that specifies a range comparison can vary from one database to another. Some DBMSs return the data that is on the row that matches the specified minimum value in addition to that on other rows up to the specified maximum value. Other DBMSs only return the data for rows that truly match between the specified minimum and maximum values.

The SQL script listed below makes a **SELECT** query that retrieves data from those rows where the value in its "price" column falls within a specified numerical range. A second **SELECT** query retrieves data from those rows where the value in its "make" column falls within a specified alphabetical ranges:

Hot tip

Refer to the documentation for your own DBMS to see how it treats the **BETWEEN** and **AND** keywords.

88

filter-range.sql

```
# Use the "my_database" database.
USE my_database ;

# Create a table called "treadmills".
CREATE TABLE IF NOT EXISTS treadmills
(
  code      CHAR( 8 )      PRIMARY KEY ,
  make      VARCHAR( 25 )  NOT NULL ,
  model     VARCHAR( 25 )  NOT NULL ,
  price     INT            NOT NULL
) ;

# Insert 5 records into the "treadmills" table.
INSERT INTO treadmills ( code , make , model , price )
  VALUES ( "335/1914"  "York"  "Pacer 2120"  159 ) ;
INSERT INTO treadmills ( code , make , model , price )
  VALUES ( "335/1907"  "York"  "Pacer 2750"  349 ) ;
```

```
INSERT INTO treadmills ( code , make , model , price )
  VALUES ( "335/1921"  "York"  "Pacer 3100"  499 ) ;
INSERT INTO treadmills ( code , make , model , price )
  VALUES ( "335/2717"  "Proform"  "7.25Q"  799 ) ;
INSERT INTO treadmills ( code , make , model , price )
  VALUES ( "335/2652"  "Reebok"  "TR1 Power Run"  895 ) ;
```

```
# Show all records where the price is between 300 - 500.
SELECT * FROM treadmills
  WHERE price BETWEEN 300 AND 500 ;
```

```
# Show records where make is between "Proform" and "York".
SELECT * FROM treadmills
  WHERE make BETWEEN "P" AND "Y" ;
```

```
# Delete this sample table.
DROP TABLE IF EXISTS treadmills ;
```

MySQL includes the data from the row matching the specified minimum value "Proform" in this example – other DBMSs may not.

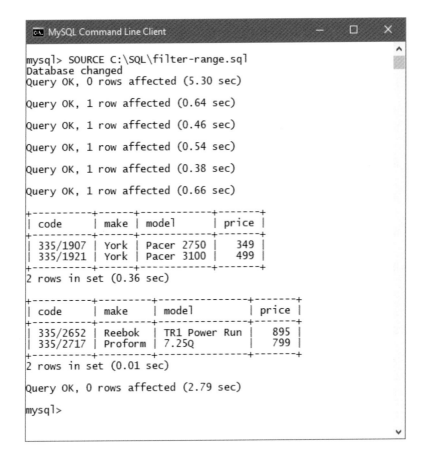

```
mysql> SOURCE C:\SQL\filter-range.sql
Database changed
Query OK, 0 rows affected (5.30 sec)

Query OK, 1 row affected (0.64 sec)

Query OK, 1 row affected (0.46 sec)

Query OK, 1 row affected (0.54 sec)

Query OK, 1 row affected (0.38 sec)

Query OK, 1 row affected (0.66 sec)

+----------+-------+-------------+-------+
| code     | make  | model       | price |
+----------+-------+-------------+-------+
| 335/1907 | York  | Pacer 2750  |   349 |
| 335/1921 | York  | Pacer 3100  |   499 |
+----------+-------+-------------+-------+
2 rows in set (0.36 sec)

+----------+---------+---------------+-------+
| code     | make    | model         | price |
+----------+---------+---------------+-------+
| 335/2652 | Reebok  | TR1 Power Run |   895 |
| 335/2717 | Proform | 7.25Q         |   799 |
+----------+---------+---------------+-------+
2 rows in set (0.01 sec)

Query OK, 0 rows affected (2.79 sec)

mysql>
```

Seeking non-matches

The != inequality operator can be used in the **WHERE** clause of a **SELECT** query to retrieve data from table rows that do not match a specified value in the tested column.

The following SQL script demonstrates how only non-matching rows can be retrieved. It first creates a table then displays its entire contents. A **SELECT** query first uses the = equality operator to display records that do match a specified value. Conversely, a final **SELECT** query uses the != inequality operator to display the other records that do not match the specified value:

filter-notequal.sql

```
# Use the "my_database" database.
USE my_database ;

# Create a table called "office_chairs".
CREATE TABLE IF NOT EXISTS office_chairs
(
  code        CHAR( 8 )      PRIMARY KEY ,
  model       VARCHAR( 25 )  NOT NULL ,
  fabric      VARCHAR( 25 )  DEFAULT "Cloth" ,
  price       DECIMAL( 6,2 ) NOT NULL
) ;

# Insert 5 records into the "office_chairs" table.
INSERT INTO office_chairs ( code , model , price )
  VALUES ( "617/9148"  "Clerk"  19.99 ) ;
INSERT INTO office_chairs ( code , model , price )
  VALUES ( "617/8156"  "Secretary"  34.99 ) ;
INSERT INTO office_chairs ( code , model , price )
  VALUES ( "617/9131"  "Manager"  "Leather"  49.99 ) ;
INSERT INTO office_chairs ( code , model , price )
  VALUES ( "621/0258"  "Captain"  "Wood"  99.99 ) ;
INSERT INTO office_chairs ( code , model , price )
  VALUES ( "619/6444"  "Executive"  "Leather"  124.99 ) ;

# Show all data in the "office_chairs" table.
SELECT * FROM office_chairs ;

# Show all records where the fabric is "Leather".
SELECT * FROM office_chairs WHERE fabric = "Leather" ;
```

\# Show all records where the fabric is not "Leather".
SELECT * FROM office_chairs WHERE fabric != "Leather" ;

\# Delete this sample table.
DROP TABLE IF EXISTS office_chairs ;

```
MySQL Command Line Client                    —    □    ×

mysql> SOURCE C:\SQL\filter-notequal.sql
Database changed
Query OK, 0 rows affected (2.17 sec)

Query OK, 1 row affected (0.34 sec)

Query OK, 1 row affected (0.15 sec)

Query OK, 1 row affected (0.18 sec)

Query OK, 1 row affected (0.13 sec)

Query OK, 1 row affected (0.18 sec)

+----------+-----------+---------+--------+
| code     | model     | fabric  | price  |
+----------+-----------+---------+--------+
| 617/8156 | Secretary | Cloth   |  34.99 |
| 617/9131 | Manager   | Leather |  49.99 |
| 617/9148 | Clerk     | Cloth   |  19.99 |
| 619/6444 | Executive | Leather | 124.99 |
| 621/0258 | Captain   | Wood    |  99.99 |
+----------+-----------+---------+--------+
5 rows in set (0.00 sec)

+----------+-----------+---------+--------+
| code     | model     | fabric  | price  |
+----------+-----------+---------+--------+
| 617/9131 | Manager   | Leather |  49.99 |
| 619/6444 | Executive | Leather | 124.99 |
+----------+-----------+---------+--------+
2 rows in set (0.05 sec)

+----------+-----------+--------+-------+
| code     | model     | fabric | price |
+----------+-----------+--------+-------+
| 617/8156 | Secretary | Cloth  | 34.99 |
| 617/9148 | Clerk     | Cloth  | 19.99 |
| 621/0258 | Captain   | Wood   | 99.99 |
+----------+-----------+--------+-------+
3 rows in set (0.00 sec)

Query OK, 0 rows affected (0.95 sec)

mysql> ▄
```

Hot tip

Unlike some other DBMSs, MySQL does not support !< "not less than" or !> "not greater than" syntax – these are simply the same as > "greater than" and < "less than" respectively.

Finding null values

The SQL keywords **IS NULL** can be used in the **WHERE** clause of a **SELECT** query to retrieve data from table records that have no value in the tested column field. Recall that the column definition must permit that column to contain empty fields.

The "color" column in the SQL example below allows a color to be optionally stored – if no color is specified, that field will contain a **NULL** value by default. An **EXPLAIN** query confirms the table format, then all that table's data is displayed. A **SELECT** query then retrieves the data from rows where no color value is stated:

filter-null.sql

Don't forget

A **NULL** value represents a completely empty field – it is not the same as zero or an "" empty string.

```
# Use the "my_database" database.
USE my_database ;

# Create a table called "steam_irons".
CREATE TABLE IF NOT EXISTS steam_irons
(
  id          INT            AUTO_INCREMENT PRIMARY KEY ,
  make        VARCHAR( 25 )  NOT NULL ,
  model       VARCHAR( 25 )  NOT NULL ,
  color       VARCHAR( 25 )
) ;

# Insert 5 records into the "steam_irons" table.
INSERT INTO steam_irons ( make , model , color )
  VALUES ( "Philips"  "GC3020"  "Lilac" ) ;
INSERT INTO steam_irons ( make , model , color )
  VALUES ( "Morphy Richards"  "40608" ) ;
INSERT INTO steam_irons ( make , model , color )
  VALUES ( "Tefal"  "1819 Avantis" ) ;
INSERT INTO steam_irons ( make , model , color )
  VALUES ( "Rowenta"  "DM529" ) ;
INSERT INTO steam_irons ( make , model , color )
  VALUES ( "Bosch"  "TDA8360"  "Blue" ) ;

# Show the table format.
EXPLAIN steam_irons ;

# Show all data in the "steam_irons" table.
SELECT * FROM steam_irons ;
```

...cont'd

Show all records where there is no specified color.
SELECT * FROM steam_irons WHERE color IS NULL ;

Delete this sample table.
DROP TABLE IF EXISTS steam_irons ;

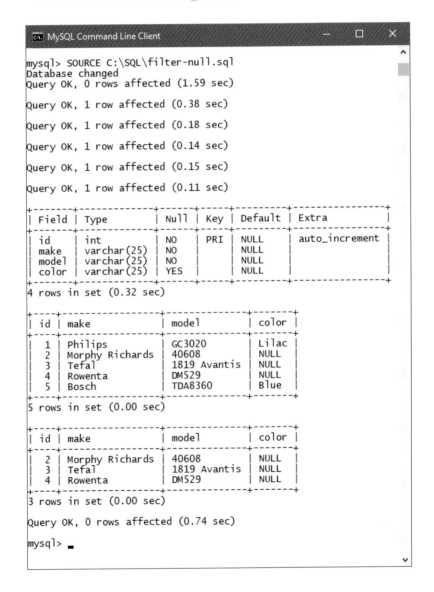

The **IS NULL** keywords must be used to match **NULL** values in a **SELECT** query – using = **NULL** does not work.

Add the **NOT** keyword to an **IS NULL** clause to match where the tested field does contain a value – for instance, **WHERE color IS NOT NULL**.

Summary

- Specific data can be retrieved from a database table by stating search criteria in a **SELECT** query.

- Search criteria are specified in the **WHERE** clause of a **SELECT** query.

- Comparison operators are used to compare the contents of the fields in a particular column against a specified value.

- A comparison is true when the evaluation succeeds and false when it fails.

- The = equality operator evaluates a comparison as true when both values match.

- The != inequality operator evaluates a comparison as true when the tested values do not match.

- A > "greater than" operator evaluates a comparison as true when the tested column value exceeds the specified value.

- A < "less than" operator evaluates a comparison as true when the tested column value is less than the specified value.

- The <= and >= operators also evaluate comparisons as true when the tested column value matches the specified value.

- A column value can be compared to a specified range of values with a **BETWEEN AND** clause.

- Search criteria can test to see if column fields are empty with both **IS NULL** and **IS NOT NULL** clauses.

- SQL comparison operators may vary from one DBMS to another – mostly adding to the basic comparison operators in this chapter.

8 Complex data filtering

This chapter builds on the previous one to demonstrate logical operators. These allow the WHERE clause in a SELECT query to stipulate multiple conditions for selecting data from a table.

Comparing multiple values

A **WHERE** clause in a **SELECT** query can make multiple comparisons using the **AND** logical operator. This enables comparisons to be made against the values contained in more than one column on each row. The syntax looks like this:

```
SELECT data FROM table-name
WHERE column = value AND column = value ;
```

The **WHERE** clause that states multiple expressions in this way will only evaluate as true when <u>all</u> comparisons evaluate as true.

In the following SQL script, a **SELECT** query has a **WHERE** clause that makes two comparisons using the **AND** operator. The data is returned only for those rows that meet both conditions:

filter-and.sql

Hot tip

The **WHERE** query could state several comparisons with multiple **AND** operators – it is not limited to just two comparisons.

```
# Use the "my_database" database.
USE my_database ;

# Create a table called "dining_sets".
CREATE TABLE IF NOT EXISTS dining_sets
(
  id        INT           AUTO_INCREMENT PRIMARY KEY ,
  model     VARCHAR( 25 ) NOT NULL ,
  color     VARCHAR( 25 ) NOT NULL ,
  price     DECIMAL( 6,2 ) NOT NULL
) ;

# Insert 5 records into the "dining_sets" table.
INSERT INTO dining_sets ( model , color , price )
  VALUES ( "Catalina" , "Cherry" , 349.99 ) ;
INSERT INTO dining_sets ( model, color, price )
  VALUES ( "Bistro" , "Silver" , 99.99 ) ;
INSERT INTO dining_sets ( model , color , price )
  VALUES ( "Michigan" , "Silver" , 179.99 ) ;
INSERT INTO dining_sets ( model , color , price )
  VALUES ( "Oregon" , "Silver" , 199.99 ) ;
INSERT INTO dining_sets ( model , color , price )
  VALUES ( "Medina" , "Black" , 159.99 ) ;
```

Show all data in the "dining_sets" table.
SELECT * FROM dining_sets ;

Show all records where the color is "Silver"
and the price is above 100.00.
SELECT * FROM dining_sets
WHERE color = "Silver" AND price > 100.00 ;

Delete this sample table.
DROP TABLE IF EXISTS dining_sets ;

```
MySQL Command Line Client                    —   □   ×

mysql> SOURCE C:\SQL\filter-and.sql
Database changed
Query OK, 0 rows affected (1.72 sec)

Query OK, 1 row affected (0.21 sec)

Query OK, 1 row affected (0.14 sec)

Query OK, 1 row affected (0.13 sec)

Query OK, 1 row affected (0.15 sec)

Query OK, 1 row affected (0.14 sec)

+----+----------+--------+--------+
| id | model    | color  | price  |
+----+----------+--------+--------+
|  1 | Catalina | Cherry | 349.99 |
|  2 | Bistro   | Silver |  99.99 |
|  3 | Michigan | Silver | 179.99 |
|  4 | Oregon   | Silver | 199.99 |
|  5 | Medina   | Black  | 159.99 |
+----+----------+--------+--------+
5 rows in set (0.00 sec)

+----+----------+--------+--------+
| id | model    | color  | price  |
+----+----------+--------+--------+
|  3 | Michigan | Silver | 179.99 |
|  4 | Oregon   | Silver | 199.99 |
+----+----------+--------+--------+
2 rows in set (0.00 sec)

Query OK, 0 rows affected (0.68 sec)

mysql> _
```

Don't forget

In this example, the "Bistro" data is not returned even though the "color" comparison is true, as the "price" comparison is false, being below 100.00.

Comparing alternative values

A **WHERE** clause in a **SELECT** query can make multiple comparisons using the **OR** logical operator. This enables comparisons to be made against the values contained in more than one column on each row. The syntax looks like this:

```
SELECT data FROM table-name
WHERE column = value OR column = value ;
```

The **WHERE** clause that states multiple conditions in this way will evaluate as true when <u>any</u> of the comparisons evaluate as true.

The following SQL script builds the same table as the previous example on pages 96-97, but now a **SELECT** query has a **WHERE** clause that makes two comparisons using the **OR** operator. The data is returned only for those rows that meet any of the conditions:

filter-or.sql

Hot tip

The **WHERE** query could state several comparisons with multiple **OR** operators – it is not limited to just two comparisons.

```
# Use the "my_database" database.
USE my_database ;

# Create a table called "dining_sets".
CREATE TABLE IF NOT EXISTS dining_sets
(
  id          INT             AUTO_INCREMENT PRIMARY KEY ,
  model       VARCHAR( 25 )   NOT NULL ,
  color       VARCHAR( 25 )   NOT NULL ,
  price       DECIMAL( 6,2 )  NOT NULL
) ;

# Insert 5 records into the "dining_sets" table.
INSERT INTO dining_sets ( model , color , price )
  VALUES ( "Catalina" , "Cherry" , 349.99 ) ;
INSERT INTO dining_sets ( model , color , price )
  VALUES ( "Bistro" , "Silver" , 99.99 ) ;
INSERT INTO dining_sets ( model , color , price )
  VALUES ( "Michigan" , "Silver" , 179.99 ) ;
INSERT INTO dining_sets ( model , color , price )
  VALUES ( "Oregon" , "Silver" , 199.99 ) ;
INSERT INTO dining_sets ( model , color , price )
  VALUES ( "Medina" , "Black" , 159.99 ) ;
```

```
# Show all data in the "dining_sets" table.
SELECT * FROM dining_sets ;

# Show all records where the color is not "Silver"
# or the price is below 100.00.
SELECT * FROM dining_sets
WHERE color != "Silver" OR price < 100.00 ;

# Delete this sample table.
DROP TABLE IF EXISTS dining_sets ;
```

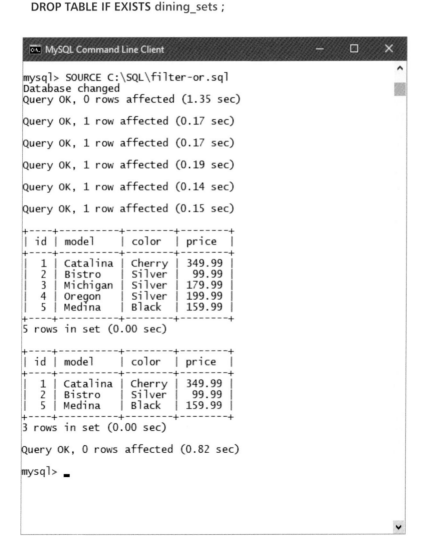

In this example, the "Catalina" and "Medina" data is returned because the "color" comparison is true; they are not "Silver". The "Bistro" data is returned because the "price" comparison is true, being below 100.00.

Comparing alternative lists

A **WHERE** clause in a **SELECT** query can specify a list of alternative values for comparison with column data using the **IN** keyword. This is followed by a comma-separated list of values within a single pair of parentheses. The syntax looks like this:

```
SELECT data FROM table-name
WHERE column IN ( value , value , value ) ;
```

When the column data matches any one of the values in the list, the **WHERE** clause evaluates as true, and data is returned for that row. The comparison can be inverted by preceding the **IN** keyword with the **NOT** keyword. Then, the **WHERE** clause only evaluates as true when no list value matches the column data.

The SQL script listed below demonstrates the comparison of multiple values using both **IN** and **NOT IN** clauses:

filter-in.sql

```
# Use the "my_database" database.
USE my_database ;

# Create a table called "coffee_makers".
CREATE TABLE IF NOT EXISTS coffee_makers
(
    id          INT            AUTO_INCREMENT PRIMARY KEY ,
    make        VARCHAR( 25 )  NOT NULL ,
    model       VARCHAR( 25 )  NOT NULL ,
    price       DECIMAL( 6,2 ) NOT NULL
) ;

# Insert 5 records into the "coffee_makers" table.
INSERT INTO coffee_makers ( make , model , price )
 VALUES ( "Cookworks" , "TSK-182" , 19.99 ) ;
INSERT INTO coffee_makers ( make , model , price )
 VALUES ( "Morphy Richards" , "Europa" , 38.25 ) ;
INSERT INTO coffee_makers ( make , model , price )
 VALUES ( "Krups" , "Vivo" , 79.50 ) ;
INSERT INTO coffee_makers ( make , model , price )
 VALUES ( "DeLonghi" , "EC410" , 139.00 ) ;
INSERT INTO coffee_makers ( make , model , price )
 VALUES ( "Gaggia" , "DeLuxe" , 199.00 ) ;
```

Show all data in the "coffee_makers" table.
SELECT * FROM coffee_makers ;

Show records where make is "Krups", "Gaggia" or
"DeLonghi" and the model is not "TSK-182" or "EC410".
SELECT * FROM coffee_makers
WHERE make IN ("Krups" , "Gaggia" , "DeLonghi")
AND model NOT IN ("TSK-182" , "EC410") ;

Delete this sample table.
DROP TABLE IF EXISTS coffee_makers ;

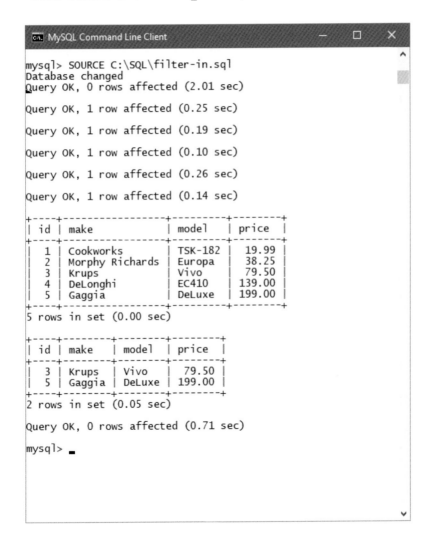

In this example, the "Krups", "Gaggia" and "DeLonghi" data is selected by the comparison to the first list. The second comparison list then excludes the "DeLonghi" data because its model value matches the second value in the comparison list.

Specifying evaluation order

The **WHERE** clause in a **SELECT** query can contain any number of comparison tests using the **AND** and **OR** keywords. But care must be taken in their use to avoid unexpected results that can be caused by the order in which the comparisons are evaluated.

The order of evaluation can be explicitly specified by surrounding an expression with ( ) parentheses – that expression then gets evaluated before anything else.

To demonstrate this problem, and its solution, the following script contains two **SELECT** queries that attempt to extract specific data. These two queries are identical, except only one explicitly specifies the evaluation order. That one returns the correct data, whereas the other one also returns a row of data erroneously:

eval-order.sql

```
# Use the "my_database" database.
USE my_database ;

# Create a table called "backpacks".
CREATE TABLE IF NOT EXISTS backpacks
(
  id          INT      AUTO_INCREMENT PRIMARY KEY ,
  make        VARCHAR( 8 ) ,
  model       VARCHAR( 25 ) ,
  price       DECIMAL( 6,2 )
) ;

# Insert 4 records into the "backpacks" table.
INSERT INTO backpacks ( make , model , price )
  VALUES ( "Adidas" , "NYC Uptown" , 17.99 ) ;
INSERT INTO backpacks ( make , model , price )
  VALUES ( "Nike", "Arrow" , 11.99 ) ;
INSERT INTO backpacks ( make , model , price )
  VALUES ( "Nike" , "Sevilla" , 13.99 ) ;
INSERT INTO backpacks ( make , model , price )
  VALUES ( "Reebok" , "Streetsport" , 11.99 ) ;

# Show all data in the "backpacks" table.
SELECT * FROM backpacks ;
```

Don't forget

By default, the **AND** operator takes precedence over the **OR** operator – expressions using **AND** get evaluated first unless parentheses are used to explicitly specify an alternative order of precedence.

```
# Show records where make is "Nike" or "Reebok"
# and price is 11.99 without explicit evaluation order.
SELECT * FROM backpacks
WHERE make = "Nike"
OR make = "Reebok" AND price = 11.99 ;

# Show records where make is "Nike" or "Reebok"
# and price is 11.99 with explicit evaluation order.
SELECT * FROM backpacks
WHERE ( make = "Nike" OR make = "Reebok" )
AND price = 11.99 ;

# Delete this sample table.
DROP TABLE IF EXISTS backpacks ;
```

```
CA. MySQL Command Line Client              —   □   ×
mysql> SOURCE C:\SQL\eval-order.sql
Database changed
Query OK, 0 rows affected (0.64 sec)

Query OK, 1 row affected (0.33 sec)

Query OK, 1 row affected (0.29 sec)

Query OK, 1 row affected (0.11 sec)

Query OK, 1 row affected (0.09 sec)

+----+--------+-------------+-------+
| id | make   | model       | price |
+----+--------+-------------+-------+
|  1 | Adidas | NYC Uptown  | 17.99 |
|  2 | Nike   | Arrow       | 11.99 |
|  3 | Nike   | Sevilla     | 13.99 |
|  4 | Reebok | Streetsport | 11.99 |
+----+--------+-------------+-------+
4 rows in set (0.00 sec)

+----+--------+-------------+-------+
| id | make   | model       | price |
+----+--------+-------------+-------+
|  2 | Nike   | Arrow       | 11.99 |
|  3 | Nike   | Sevilla     | 13.99 |
|  4 | Reebok | Streetsport | 11.99 |
+----+--------+-------------+-------+
3 rows in set (0.00 sec)

+----+--------+-------------+-------+
| id | make   | model       | price |
+----+--------+-------------+-------+
|  2 | Nike   | Arrow       | 11.99 |
|  4 | Reebok | Streetsport | 11.99 |
+----+--------+-------------+-------+
2 rows in set (0.00 sec)

Query OK, 0 rows affected (0.55 sec)

mysql> _
```

Hot tip

Always use parentheses to explicitly specify the evaluation order in any **WHERE** clause that includes both **AND** and **OR** keywords.

Matching strings

Making comparisons against text strings with the SQL comparison operators will only return data when the column's text data exactly matches the specified comparison text. This is not flexible and requires knowledge of the precise content of the column field.

The **LIKE** keyword offers an alternative way to make comparisons against text strings without requiring an exact complete match. This compares a "search pattern", comprising text and one or more wildcards, against the column string. Its syntax is like this:

```
SELECT data FROM table-name
WHERE column LIKE search-pattern ;
```

Each wildcard replaces part of the original string to allow comparison of just the text element. The most common wildcard is "%", which can precede and/or follow literal text to be compared. It matches zero, one, or more characters at the point where it appears in the search pattern. For instance, "%red carpet%" could be used to match any compared column that contained the string "red carpet", regardless of any other text before or after that string.

The following SQL script creates a table populated with differing values in its "type" column. These are compared against a search pattern, and the query returns data for the row whose compared column successfully matched against that search pattern:

```
# Use the "my_database" database.
USE my_database ;
```

```
# Create a table called "shredders".
CREATE TABLE IF NOT EXISTS shredders
(
  model      VARCHAR( 8 )    PRIMARY KEY ,
  type       VARCHAR( 25 )   DEFAULT "strip cut" ,
  price      DECIMAL( 6,2 )
) ;
```

```
# Insert 4 records into the "shredders" table.
INSERT INTO shredders ( model , price )
  VALUES ( "PS60" , 64.99 ) ;
```

Hot tip

Some DBMSs, such as Access, use the "*" character in place of the "%" wildcard.

match-strings.sql

```
INSERT INTO shredders ( model , price )
  VALUES ( "PS70" , 99.99 ) ;
INSERT INTO shredders ( model , type , price )
  VALUES ( "PS400" , "cross cut" , 64.99 ) ;
INSERT INTO shredders ( model , price )
  VALUES ( "PS500" , 29.95 ) ;

# Show all data in the "shredders" table.
SELECT * FROM shredders ;

# Show records where the model is a "cross cut" type.
SELECT * FROM shredders WHERE type LIKE "%cross%" ;

# Delete this sample table.
DROP TABLE IF EXISTS shredders ;
```

Don't forget

Search patterns, like all other text strings, must be enclosed within quotes – including any wildcard characters.

Matching characters

The "%" wildcard represents zero, one, or more characters in a search pattern. Another wildcard is the "_" underscore character that always represents just a single character in a search pattern.

The "_" wildcard is used in the same way as the "%" wildcard, and can appear several times in a single search pattern to represent multiple characters. It can also be used alongside the "%" wildcard in a search pattern. For instance, the search pattern "t_b%" would seek to match any string beginning with a "t" whose third letter is "b" regardless of any following characters.

The following example uses the "_" wildcard to represent the third, fifth and sixth characters in a search pattern. These are compared with the string values in the table's "name" column – in this case, there are two strings that match the search pattern:

match-chars.sql

Hot tip

Some DBMSs, such as Access, use the "?" character in place of the "_" wildcard.

```
# Use the "my_database" database.
USE my_database ;
```

```
# Create a table called "glass_sets".
CREATE TABLE IF NOT EXISTS glass_sets
(
  id       INT           AUTO_INCREMENT PRIMARY KEY ,
  name     VARCHAR( 25 ) NOT NULL ,
  price    DECIMAL( 6,2 ) NOT NULL
) ;
```

```
# Insert 5 records into the "glass_sets" table.
INSERT INTO glass_sets ( name , price )
  VALUES ( "Monaco" , 6.99 ) ;
INSERT INTO glass_sets ( name , price )
  VALUES ( "Cavendish" , 4.99 ) ;
INSERT INTO glass_sets ( name , price )
  VALUES ( "Mosaic" , 6.99 ) ;
INSERT INTO glass_sets ( name , price )
  VALUES ( "Blue Reef" , 8.99 ) ;
INSERT INTO glass_sets ( name , price )
  VALUES ( "Silver Swirl" , 14.99 ) ;
```

```
# Show all data in the "glass_sets" table.
SELECT * FROM glass_sets;
```

```
# Show records where the name matches a search pattern.
SELECT * FROM glass_sets WHERE name LIKE "mo_a__" ;
```

```
MySQL Command Line Client                    —    □    ×

mysql> SOURCE C:\SQL\match-chars.sql
Database changed
Query OK, 0 rows affected (0.95 sec)

Query OK, 1 row affected (0.08 sec)

Query OK, 1 row affected (0.18 sec)

Query OK, 1 row affected (0.15 sec)

Query OK, 1 row affected (0.09 sec)

Query OK, 1 row affected (0.10 sec)

+----+-------------+-------+
| id | name        | price |
+----+-------------+-------+
|  1 | Monaco      |  6.99 |
|  2 | Cavendish   |  4.99 |
|  3 | Mosaic      |  6.99 |
|  4 | Blue Reef   |  8.99 |
|  5 | Silver Swirl| 14.99 |
+----+-------------+-------+
5 rows in set (0.00 sec)

+----+--------+-------+
| id | name   | price |
+----+--------+-------+
|  1 | Monaco |  6.99 |
|  3 | Mosaic |  6.99 |
+----+--------+-------+
2 rows in set (0.00 sec)

mysql> _
```

Remember that the "_" wildcard always matches exactly one character.

107

This SQL example does not delete the "glass_sets" table so it can be used to demonstrate further comparison queries by the example on pages 108-109.

Matching regular expressions

Powerful search patterns can be specified as "regular expressions" using the **REGEXP** keyword. These can add special characters to text in the search pattern to denote their significance. The table below contains some common examples of regular expressions:

Regular Expression	Matches
"A"	A single character – here, it's any string containing a letter A
"[ABC]"	A list of characters – here, it's any string containing one of the letters A or B or C
"[A-K]"	A range of characters – here, it's any string containing one of the letters A through K
"[0-5]"	A range of digits – here, it's any string containing one of the digits 0 through 5
"^M"	A single character at the beginning of the string – here, it's any string starting with the letter M
"H$"	A single character at the end of the string – here, it's any string ending with the letter H

Beware

Support for regular expressions does vary from one DBMS to another. In MySQL they are not case sensitive – so the expression "A" would match any string containing a letter "A" in either uppercase or lowercase.

108

The following SQL script queries the "glass_sets" table that was created in the previous example on pages 106-107. It matches a number of regular expressions to strings contained in the "name" column:

SQL

match-regexp.sql

```
# Show records where the name contains a "W".
SELECT * FROM glass_sets WHERE name REGEXP "W" ;

# Show records where the name contains a "W" or a "N".
SELECT * FROM glass_sets WHERE name REGEXP "[WN]" ;

# Show records where the name begins with a "B".
SELECT * FROM glass_sets WHERE name REGEXP "^B" ;

# Show records where the name ends with a "H".
SELECT * FROM glass_sets WHERE name REGEXP "H$" ;
```

...cont'd

Show records where the name begins with a "B" or "C".
SELECT * FROM glass_sets WHERE name REGEXP "^[BC]" ;

Now delete this sample table.
DROP TABLE IF EXISTS glass_sets ;

```
MySQL Command Line Client                              —    □    ×

mysql> SOURCE C:\SQL\match-regexp.sql
+----+-------------+-------+
| id | name        | price |
+----+-------------+-------+
|  5 | Silver Swirl | 14.99 |
+----+-------------+-------+
1 row in set (0.43 sec)

+----+-------------+-------+
| id | name        | price |
+----+-------------+-------+
|  1 | Monaco      |  6.99 |
|  2 | Cavendish   |  4.99 |
|  5 | Silver Swirl | 14.99 |
+----+-------------+-------+
3 rows in set (0.00 sec)

+----+-----------+-------+
| id | name      | price |
+----+-----------+-------+
|  4 | Blue Reef |  8.99 |
+----+-----------+-------+
1 row in set (0.01 sec)

+----+-----------+-------+
| id | name      | price |
+----+-----------+-------+
|  2 | Cavendish |  4.99 |
+----+-----------+-------+
1 row in set (0.00 sec)

+----+-----------+-------+
| id | name      | price |
+----+-----------+-------+
|  2 | Cavendish |  4.99 |
|  4 | Blue Reef |  8.99 |
+----+-----------+-------+
2 rows in set (0.00 sec)

Query OK, 0 rows affected (1.63 sec)

mysql> _
```

Hot tip

Single characters can be matched in a regular expression by a dot. For instance, "^....$" would match any string that contains exactly four characters.

Hot tip

Put the NOT keyword before the REGEXP keyword to return all strings that <u>don't</u> match the expression.

Summary

- The logical **AND** operator can be added to a **WHERE** clause in a **SELECT** query to allow comparisons against multiple columns.

- All multiple **AND** comparisons must evaluate as true in order for the **WHERE** clause to return data from the current row.

- The logical **OR** operator can be added to a **WHERE** clause in a **SELECT** query to allow comparisons against multiple columns.

- Any one of the multiple **OR** comparisons must evaluate as true for the **WHERE** clause to return data from the current row.

- A **WHERE** clause can specify a comma-separated list of alternative comparison values in parentheses following the **IN** keyword.

- Data can be returned from rows that do <u>not</u> match any of the list of values by adding a **NOT** keyword before the **IN** keyword.

- Both logical **AND** and **OR** operators can be added to a single **WHERE** clause to allow comparisons against multiple columns.

- The **AND** operator is evaluated before the **OR** operator.

- Parentheses should be added to **WHERE** clauses that contain both **AND** and **OR** operators to specify the evaluation order.

- The **LIKE** operator can be added to a **WHERE** clause to specify a search pattern for comparison against a string value.

- A "%" wildcard represents zero, one, or more characters in a search pattern.

- A "_" wildcard represents just one character in a search pattern.

- Search patterns may contain multiple instances of the "%" and "_" wildcards.

- The **REGEXP** keyword can be used in a **WHERE** clause to specify a regular expression for comparison against a string value.

- Data can be returned from rows that do <u>not</u> match a regular expression using the **NOT REGEXP** keywords.

9 Generating calculated fields

This chapter demonstrates how to create and utilize calculated fields within a database table.

Concatenating fields

A "calculated field" is created using data stored within several columns of a database. It does not form an additional column in the table, but is generated dynamically to display the result of a calculation that uses data from existing fields.

Calculated fields are useful to present a range of data in a formatted manner. For instance, a table may typically store address data in separate columns for street, city, state and zip code, but a mailing program needs this data to be retrieved as a single formatted field. This requires the data stored in the various columns to be concatenated (joined together) to form a single calculated field.

The technique to concatenate string data varies by DBMS, but usually a formatting separator is placed between each piece of data. This typically may be a space, comma or newline character.

Some DBMSs, such as those from Microsoft, favor concatenation using the "+" operator, with this syntax:

Don't forget

Consult the documentation of your DBMS to discover which type of concatenation it supports.

```
calculated-field = column1 + separator + column2
```

The "+" operator in this case recognizes the column data type as text, so it attempts to concatenate the strings – rather than attempt a numerical addition. Other databases, such as Oracle, favor the "||" operator for concatenation in place of the "+" character.

MySQL has a special **CONCAT** keyword for this purpose that allows the columns to be concatenated to be specified as a comma-separated list within parentheses after this keyword. For concatenation with a designated separator it also has a similar **CONCAT_WS** keyword that automatically recognizes the first item in the list as a separator to include between each piece of data. The syntax for this concatenation feature looks like this:

Hot tip

CONCAT_WS means "Concatenate With Separator".

```
CONCAT_WS ( separator , column1 , column2 )
```

The SQL script on the opposite page demonstrates the creation of calculated fields with both **CONCAT** and **CONCAT_WS**.

...cont'd

concat.sql

```sql
# Use the "my_database" database.
USE my_database ;

# Create a table called "hotels".
CREATE TABLE IF NOT EXISTS hotels
(
  name          VARCHAR( 25 )   PRIMARY KEY ,
  street        VARCHAR( 25 ) ,
  city          VARCHAR( 25 ) ,
  state         VARCHAR( 25 ) ,
  zip           INT
) ;

# Insert a record into the "hotels" table.
INSERT INTO hotels ( name , street , city , state , zip )
  VALUES ( "Las Vegas Hilton" , "3000 Paradise Road" ,
              "Las Vegas" , "Nevada" , 89109 ) ;

# Retrieve 2 concatenated calculated fields.
SELECT CONCAT( name , ", " , state ) FROM hotels ;
SELECT CONCAT_WS( ",\n" , name , street , city , state , zip )
FROM hotels ;

# Delete this sample table.
DROP TABLE IF EXISTS hotels ;
```

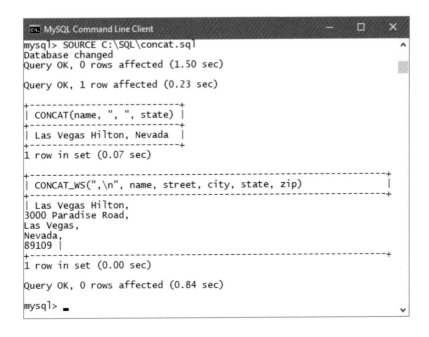

Hot tip

In this example, **CONCAT** adds a comma and a space separator, whereas **CONCAT_WS** adds a comma and a "\n" newline separator between each item of data.

Trimming padded spaces

Some databases automatically add spaces to strings to pad them out to the column width. For instance, with a column data type of **VARCHAR(10)**, a five-letter string might have five trailing spaces added to pad it out to the full column width.

Padded strings do not usually present a problem when retrieving single items of data, but they are not desirable when concatenating several strings into a calculated field.

All leading and trailing spaces can be removed from a string with the **TRIM** keyword. The name of the column to be trimmed should follow this keyword within parentheses, like this:

TRIM (*column*)

Most DBMSs also support **LTRIM** and **RTRIM** keywords that trim spaces from the left and right of the string respectively.

MySQL does not automatically pad strings with spaces to the column width, but strings that are stored with leading and/or trailing spaces can be trimmed with the **TRIM** keyword.

The following example SQL script creates a table populated with string values that deliberately have both leading and trailing spaces. The strings are trimmed by each **SELECT** query to return concatenated calculated fields:

trim.sql

```
# Use the "my_database" database.
USE my_database ;

# Create a table called "padded".
CREATE TABLE IF NOT EXISTS padded
(
  id            INT      AUTO_INCREMENT PRIMARY KEY ,
  str1          CHAR( 10 ) ,
  str2          CHAR( 10 ) ,
  str3          CHAR( 10 )
) ;

# Insert 2 records into the "padded" table.
INSERT INTO padded ( str1 , str2 , str3 )
  VALUES ( " MySQL   " , " Data    " , " Bases   " ) ;
```

```
INSERT INTO padded ( str1 , str2 , str3 )
 VALUES ( " are     " , " great    " , " fun !   " ) ;
```

```
# Show all data in the "padded" table.
SELECT * FROM padded ;
```

```
# Retrieve 2 trimmed concatenated calculated fields.
SELECT CONCAT( TRIM( str1 ) , RTRIM( str2 ) , LTRIM( str3 ) )
FROM padded WHERE id = 1 ;
```

```
SELECT CONCAT( TRIM( str1 ) , RTRIM( str2 ) , TRIM( str3 ) )
FROM padded WHERE id = 2 ;
```

```
# Delete this sample table.
DROP TABLE IF EXISTS padded ;
```

Hot tip

This example uses a combination of **TRIM**, **LTRIM** and **RTRIM** to format the strings as required.

Adopting aliases

In the previous examples in this chapter, the heading of each calculated field simply displays the code that created that field. It is often preferable to assign a meaningful heading to label the calculated field instead – in the same way that a column header labels a regular column. This label is known as an "alias" and is specified by the **AS** keyword in a **SELECT** query.

If an alias is to include spaces, it should be enclosed within quotes when specified by the **AS** keyword – a single word alias does not need quotes around it.

The following SQL script creates and populates a table then generates two calculated fields, each labeled with an alias. Note that the **EXPLAIN** query confirms that the calculated field is only generated as output, and is not actually added to the table:

SQL

alias.sql

Hot tip

Aliases can also be used to dynamically replace a column header in output. This does not change the name given to the column – only the label in the **SELECT** query response output.

```
# Use the "my_database" database.
USE my_database ;

# Create a table called "fishermans_wharf".
CREATE TABLE IF NOT EXISTS fishermans_wharf
(
  street      VARCHAR( 20 )  PRIMARY KEY ,
  city        CHAR( 20 )     DEFAULT "San Francisco" ,
  state       CHAR( 2 )      DEFAULT "CA" ,
  zip         INT            DEFAULT 94133
) ;

# Insert 2 records into the "fishermans_wharf" table.
INSERT INTO fishermans_wharf ( street )
  VALUES ( "145 Jefferson St." ) ;
INSERT INTO fishermans_wharf ( street )
  VALUES ( "175 Jefferson St." ) ;

# Show all data in the "fishermans_wharf" table.
SELECT * FROM fishermans_wharf ;

# Retrieve 2 concatenated calculated fields.
SELECT CONCAT_WS( ", " , street , city , state , zip )
AS Wax_Museum
FROM fishermans_wharf
WHERE street = "145 Jefferson St." ;
```

...cont'd

```
SELECT CONCAT_WS( ", " , street , city , state , zip )
AS "Ripley's Believe It Or Not! Museum"
FROM fishermans_wharf
WHERE street = "175 Jefferson St." ;
```

```
# Display the table format.
EXPLAIN fishermans_wharf ;
```

```
# Delete this sample table.
DROP TABLE IF EXISTS fishermans_wharf ;
```

```
▣ MySQL Command Line Client                       —   □   ×

mysql> SOURCE C:\SQL\alias.sql
Database changed
Query OK, 0 rows affected (1.00 sec)

Query OK, 1 row affected (0.14 sec)

Query OK, 1 row affected (0.24 sec)

+--------------------+---------------+-------+-------+
| street             | city          | state | zip   |
+--------------------+---------------+-------+-------+
| 145 Jefferson St.  | San Francisco | CA    | 94133 |
| 175 Jefferson St.  | San Francisco | CA    | 94133 |
+--------------------+---------------+-------+-------+
2 rows in set (0.00 sec)

+--------------------------------------------+
| Wax_Museum                                 |
+--------------------------------------------+
| 145 Jefferson St., San Francisco, CA, 94133 |
+--------------------------------------------+
1 row in set (0.00 sec)

+--------------------------------------------+
| Ripley's Believe It Or Not! Museum         |
+--------------------------------------------+
| 175 Jefferson St., San Francisco, CA, 94133 |
+--------------------------------------------+
1 row in set (0.00 sec)

+--------+------------+------+-----+---------------+-------+
| Field  | Type       | Null | Key | Default       | Extra |
+--------+------------+------+-----+---------------+-------+
| street | varchar(20)| NO   | PRI | NULL          |       |
| city   | char(20)   | YES  |     | San Francisco |       |
| state  | char(2)    | YES  |     | CA            |       |
| zip    | int        | YES  |     | 94133         |       |
+--------+------------+------+-----+---------------+-------+
4 rows in set (0.18 sec)

Query OK, 0 rows affected (0.42 sec)

mysql> ▁
```

Beware

Aliases that contain strings can sometimes cause problems in certain client applications. Although legal, it is better to use single word aliases or to link the words with the underscore character – as seen in this example.

Doing arithmetic

Perhaps the most useful aspect of calculated fields is to perform arithmetical operations on existing data and present the result of the calculation in a newly-generated field. SQL provides the standard arithmetical operators, listed in the table below:

Operator	Operation
+	Addition
–	Subtraction
*	Multiplication
/	Division

This SQL script example uses arithmetical operators to calculate data to be entered into calculated fields. It first creates a table then populates two of its columns with numerical data for "price" and "quantity".

The **SELECT** query in this example generates a calculated field, named "subtotal", to store the result of multiplying the price and quantity values on each row. It also generates a second calculated field, named "tax", to store the result of multiplying the subtotal on each row by 6%. A third calculated field, named "total", stores the result of adding the "subtotal" and "tax" on each row to produce a grand total:

calculate.sql

```
# Use the "my_database" database.
USE my_database ;

# Create a table called "wines".
CREATE TABLE IF NOT EXISTS wines
(
  id          INT      AUTO_INCREMENT     PRIMARY KEY ,
  type        CHAR( 10 )     NOT NULL ,
  price       DECIMAL( 6,2 )  NOT NULL ,
  quantity    INT            DEFAULT 0
) ;
```

```
# Insert 3 records into the "wines" table.
INSERT INTO wines ( type , price , quantity )
  VALUES ( "Red" , 10.00 , 12 ) ;

INSERT INTO wines ( type , price , quantity )
  VALUES ( "White" , 9.00 , 12 ) ;

INSERT INTO wines ( type , price , quantity )
  VALUES ( "Rose" , 8.00 , 6 ) ;

# Generate calculated fields.
SELECT          type ,
                price AS bottle ,
                quantity AS qty ,
                price * quantity AS subtotal ,
                ( price * quantity ) * ( 6 / 100 ) AS tax ,
                ( price * quantity ) +
                ( price * quantity ) * ( 6 / 100 ) AS total
FROM wines ;

# Delete this sample table.
DROP TABLE wines ;
```

```
C:\ MySQL Command Line Client                    —    □   ✕

mysql> SOURCE C:\SQL\calculate.sql
Database changed
Query OK, 0 rows affected (1.32 sec)

Query OK, 1 row affected (0.13 sec)

Query OK, 1 row affected (0.21 sec)

Query OK, 1 row affected (0.23 sec)

+-------+--------+------+----------+----------+------------+
| type  | bottle | qty  | subtotal | tax      | total      |
+-------+--------+------+----------+----------+------------+
| Red   |  10.00 |  12  |   120.00 | 7.200000 | 127.200000 |
| White |   9.00 |  12  |   108.00 | 6.480000 | 114.480000 |
| Rose  |   8.00 |   6  |    48.00 | 2.880000 |  50.880000 |
+-------+--------+------+----------+----------+------------+
3 rows in set (0.09 sec)

Query OK, 0 rows affected (0.77 sec)

mysql> _
```

Hot tip

In this example, the "quantity" column has been given the alias of "qty" just to reduce that column's width.

Summary

● A "calculated field" is generated dynamically to display the result of a calculation that uses data from existing fields.

● Multiple strings can be concatenated into one single string.

● The methods of concatenating strings varies according to the DBMS specifications.

● Some DBMSs use the "+" operator for concatenation; others use the "||" operator.

● MySQL uses special **CONCAT** and **CONCAT_WS** keywords for concatenating strings.

● The strings to be concatenated are specified as a comma-separated list within parentheses after the **CONCAT** or **CONCAT_WS** keywords.

● **CONCAT_WS** recognizes the first item in its specified list as a separator that it automatically inserts between each string.

● Trailing and leading spaces can be removed from strings with the **TRIM, LTRIM,** and **RTRIM** keywords.

● An alias is a meaningful label that is assigned to a calculated field using the **AS** keyword in a **SELECT** query.

● The regular column heading can be replaced by an alias in the output from a **SELECT** query.

● Arithmetical operations can be performed on numerical data using the "+", "-", "*" and "/" arithmetical operators.

● The result of arithmetical operations on existing data can usefully be displayed in a newly-generated calculated field.

10 Manipulating data

This chapter demonstrates SQL functions that allow data types to be converted and data to be manipulated.

Introducing functions

An SQL function is a keyword that performs a particular preordained operation on a specified piece of data. The data is specified within parentheses following the keyword. This may be a single item or a comma-separated list – depending on the nature of the function. These are known as the function "arguments".

In Chapter 9, **CONCAT()**, **CONCAT_WS()**, **TRIM()**, **RTRIM()**, and **LTRIM()** are all SQL functions – each performing a particular task on the data specified within their parentheses.

The four types of SQL functions are listed in the following table together with a description of what they do:

Function Type	Description
Text functions	Used to manipulate strings of text. For instance, trimming spaces and converting to uppercase or lowercase
Numeric functions	Used to perform mathematical operations. For instance, returning an absolute value or calculating an algebraic expression
Date functions	Used to manipulate date and time values. For instance, returning the current time and calculating the difference between two dates
System functions	Used to return information about the DBMS itself. For instance, the version number, user information and connection number

All DBMSs provide SQL functions for the most useful operations but, unfortunately, the function names and syntax vary from one DBMS to another. This means that SQL code containing function calls is not portable between various DBMSs.

The following table lists some common function operations together with their relevant function names on some of the most popular DBMSs:

Operation	Oracle	SQL Server	MySQL
Return part of a string	SUBSTR()	SUBSTRING()	SUBSTRING()
Convert a data type	TO_CHAR() TO_NUMBER()	CONVERT()	CONVERT()
Return a rounded-up number	CEIL()	CEILING()	CEILING()
Return the current date	SYSDATE	GETDATE()	CURDATE()

Because of these differences, some programmers opt to avoid SQL functions in favor of having their program perform the required operation on the data. This enables the program to be portable across various DBMSs, but is generally less efficient.

SQL functions within a DBMS are optimized for maximum efficiency and should be used wherever possible rather than have an application perform the required operation.

The examples in the rest of this chapter feature SQL functions that are supported by MySQL. For other DBMSs, the equivalent function name and syntax must be substituted – refer to the documentation for your DBMS to discover the equivalent function name and syntax in each case.

Text functions

A section of textual data can be extracted with the **SUBSTRING()** function. This requires three arguments to be specified within its parentheses – stating the string, the character position at which to begin the substring, and the length of the substring. Its syntax is:

> SUBSTRING (*string* , *position* , *length*)

A string can be returned in uppercase with the **UPPER()** function, or in lowercase with the **LOWER()** function. The number of characters in a string can be returned using the **LENGTH()** function. String data values that sound similar can be returned using the **SOUNDEX()** function. This uses an algorithm to return an alphanumeric pattern that is a phonetic representation of the string. The pattern allows for characters and syllables that sound alike – so strings may be compared by how they sound, rather than how they are written. Each of these functions just require the string to be specified within its parentheses.

The following SQL script example returns substrings, uppercase and lowercase versions, string lengths and patterns:

Don't forget

Function names and syntax do vary on different DBMSs – see the documentation of your DBMS for its supported functions.

str-fcn.sql

```
# Use the "my_database" database.
USE my_database ;

# Create a table called "party".
CREATE TABLE IF NOT EXISTS party
(
  id        INT     AUTO_INCREMENT PRIMARY KEY ,
  dept      CHAR( 10 ) ,
  name      CHAR( 25 )
) ;

# Insert 3 records into the "party" table.
INSERT INTO party ( dept , name )
  VALUES ( "accounts" , "Graham Miller" ) ;
INSERT INTO party ( dept , name )
  VALUES ( "sales" , "Gary Miller" ) ;
INSERT INTO party ( dept , name )
  VALUES ( "production" , "Graham Wallace" ) ;

# Get 3-letter substrings from the dept column.
SELECT SUBSTRING( dept , 1 , 3 ) FROM party ;
```

...cont'd

```
# Get both cases name and length in the production dept.
SELECT UPPER( name ) , LOWER( name ) , LENGTH( name )
FROM party WHERE dept = "production" ;
```

```
# Get pattern and names that sound like "Gary Miller".
SELECT SOUNDEX( name ) , name FROM party
WHERE SOUNDEX( name ) = SOUNDEX( "Gary Miller" ) ;
```

```
# Delete this sample table.
DROP TABLE IF EXISTS party ;
```

```
mysql> SOURCE C:\SQL\str-fcn.sql
Database changed
Query OK, 0 rows affected (2.64 sec)

Query OK, 1 row affected (0.34 sec)

Query OK, 1 row affected (0.34 sec)

Query OK, 1 row affected (0.24 sec)

+----------------------+
| SUBSTRING(dept, 1, 3) |
+----------------------+
| acc                  |
| sal                  |
| pro                  |
+----------------------+
3 rows in set (0.05 sec)

+---------------+---------------+--------------+
| UPPER(name)   | LOWER(name)   | LENGTH(name) |
+---------------+---------------+--------------+
| GRAHAM WALLACE | graham wallace |           14 |
+---------------+---------------+--------------+
1 row in set (0.12 sec)

+--------------+---------------+
| SOUNDEX(name) | name          |
+--------------+---------------+
| G6546        | Graham Miller |
| G6546        | Gary Miller   |
+--------------+---------------+
2 rows in set (0.09 sec)

Query OK, 0 rows affected (1.23 sec)

mysql> _
```

Hot tip

Notice that the **SOUNDEX()** pattern is identical for both these names.

Numeric functions

SQL provides a number of standard functions for mathematical calculation – these are generally standard on all DBMSs. Some of the most useful math functions are listed in the table below:

Function	Returns
ABS(x)	Absolute value of x
COS(x)	Cosine of x, where x is given in radians
EXP(x)	Exponential value of x
MOD(x , y)	Remainder of x divided by y
PI()	3.141593
RADIANS(x)	Degrees x converted to radians
SIN(x)	Sine of x where x is given in radians
SQRT(x)	Square root of x
TAN(x)	Tangent of x where x is given in radians
FLOOR(x)	Nearest integer value below x
CEILING(x)	Nearest integer value above x
ROUND(x)	Nearest integer above or below x
RAND()	Random number in the range 0 to 1.0

The modulus function, **MOD()**, is useful to determine if a specified value is odd or even – dividing the value by 2 returns 1 for odd numbers and zero for even numbers.

Floating-point numbers can easily be rounded up to the nearest integer with the **CEILING()** function, or rounded down to the nearest integer with the **FLOOR()** function.

The example SQL script on the opposite page demonstrates some of the above functions in action and illustrates how the random floating-point value returned by the **RAND()** function can be translated to a more useful integer value in the range of 1 to 100.

Hot tip

Some DBMSs support other math functions in addition to those listed here – refer to the documentation for your DBMS to discover them.

Get some square roots.
SELECT SQRT(144) , SQRT(125) , ROUND(SQRT(125)) ;

Get Pi and round it up and down.
SELECT PI() , CEILING(PI()) , FLOOR(PI()) ;

Get some random numbers.
SELECT RAND() , RAND() ;

Get some random numbers in the range 1-100.
SELECT CEILING(RAND() * 100) , CEILING(RAND() * 100) ;

math-fcn.sql

```
MySQL Command Line Client                           —  □  ×

mysql> SOURCE C:\SQL\math-fcn.sql
+-----------+----------------------+------------------+
| SQRT(144) | SQRT(125)            | ROUND(SQRT(125)) |
+-----------+----------------------+------------------+
|        12 | 11.180339887498949   |               11 |
+-----------+----------------------+------------------+
1 row in set (0.06 sec)

+----------+--------------+-------------+
| PI()     | CEILING(PI()) | FLOOR(PI()) |
+----------+--------------+-------------+
| 3.141593 |            4 |           3 |
+----------+--------------+-------------+
1 row in set (0.08 sec)

+----------------------+----------------------+
| RAND()               | RAND()               |
+----------------------+----------------------+
| 0.02027147637705456  | 0.33162149165908011  |
+----------------------+----------------------+
1 row in set (0.00 sec)

+----------------------+----------------------+
| CEILING(RAND() * 100) | CEILING(RAND() * 100) |
+----------------------+----------------------+
|                   60 |                  100 |
+----------------------+----------------------+
1 row in set (0.00 sec)

mysql> _
```

Date and time functions

Dates and times are stored in SQL database tables as **DATE**, **TIME**, or **DATETIME** data types. These have specific formats to store the seconds, minutes, hours, day, month, and year components of a date and time in an ordered manner.

Each component of a stored date or time can be retrieved individually using an SQL function that specifies the date or time within its parentheses. **SECOND()**, **MINUTE()**, and **HOUR()** return the relevant time components. **DAYOFMONTH()**, **MONTHNAME()**, and **YEAR()** return the relevant date components. Additionally, the day's name can be returned with the **DAYNAME()** function.

The full current date and time can be returned with the **NOW()** function. The current date can be returned by the **CURDATE()** function, and the current time by the **CURTIME()** function.

This example first returns the current date and time information. It then retrieves the individual date and time components from a **DATETIME** data type in the format YYYY-MM-DD HH:MM:SS:

Don't forget

Refer back to the data type table on page 38 for date and time formats.

SQL

date-fcn.sql

Beware

Date and time functions vary greatly on different DBMSs – see the documentation of your DBMS for its date and time functions.

```
# Get the current full date object, current date & time.
SELECT NOW() , CURDATE() , CURTIME() ;
```

```
# Use the my_database database.
USE my_database ;
```

```
# Create a table called "labor_day".
CREATE TABLE IF NOT EXISTS labor_day
(
 id        INT        AUTO_INCREMENT PRIMARY KEY ,
 date      DATETIME   NOT NULL
) ;
```

```
# Insert 1 record into the "labor_day" table.
INSERT INTO labor_day ( date )
VALUES ( "2025-09-05 12:45:30" ) ;
```

```
# Get the name of the day.
SELECT DAYNAME( date ) FROM labor_day ;
```

```
# Get the day, month and year date components.
SELECT DAYOFMONTH( date ) , MONTHNAME( date ) ,YEAR( date )
FROM labor_day ;

# Get the hour, minute and second time components.
SELECT HOUR( date ) , MINUTE( date ) , SECOND( date )
FROM labor_day ;

# Delete this sample table.
DROP TABLE IF EXISTS labor_day ;
```

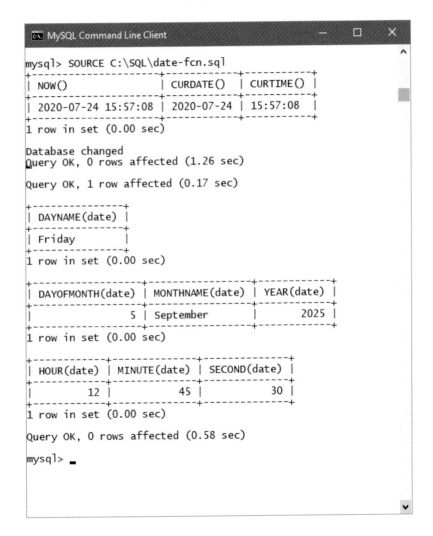

```
mysql> SOURCE C:\SQL\date-fcn.sql
+----------------------+------------+-----------+
| NOW()                | CURDATE()  | CURTIME() |
+----------------------+------------+-----------+
| 2020-07-24 15:57:08  | 2020-07-24 | 15:57:08  |
+----------------------+------------+-----------+
1 row in set (0.00 sec)

Database changed
Query OK, 0 rows affected (1.26 sec)

Query OK, 1 row affected (0.17 sec)

+----------------+
| DAYNAME(date)  |
+----------------+
| Friday         |
+----------------+
1 row in set (0.00 sec)

+-------------------+------------------+-------------+
| DAYOFMONTH(date)  | MONTHNAME(date)  | YEAR(date)  |
+-------------------+------------------+-------------+
|                5  | September        |       2025  |
+-------------------+------------------+-------------+
1 row in set (0.00 sec)

+-------------+---------------+---------------+
| HOUR(date)  | MINUTE(date)  | SECOND(date)  |
+-------------+---------------+---------------+
|         12  |           45  |           30  |
+-------------+---------------+---------------+
1 row in set (0.00 sec)

Query OK, 0 rows affected (0.58 sec)

mysql> _
```

Hot tip

Use the **BETWEEN** and **AND** keywords to match a range of dates.

Hot tip

There is also a **MONTH()** function that returns the month number in the range of 1-12.

System functions

MySQL provides a number of SQL functions and keywords to administer the database system internally. The **VERSION()** function simply returns the version number of the DBMS and the **USER()** function displays the name and domain of the user.

Each access to the database runs in an individual process known as a "thread". The **SHOW PROCESSLIST** statement will reveal the identity number of each thread. Any individual thread can be terminated by specifying its identity number within the parentheses of the **KILL()** function.

New database users can be added with a **GRANT** statement that specifies their level of activity privileges. A typical **GRANT** statement that adds a new user with password-required access and full privileges looks like this:

Don't forget

Log into MySQL as the root user, or as a user with all privileges, to be allowed to make **GRANT** statements. Type "quit" to log out of the MySQL monitor, then type **"mysql -u root"** to log back in as root.

```
GRANT ALL PRIVILEGES ON *.* TO 'user'@'domain'
IDENTIFIED BY 'password' WITH GRANT OPTION ;
```

The level of privileges granted to a user can be inspected with a **SHOW GRANTS FOR** statement, specifying the user name.

The SQL script below first displays the MySQL version number and current user. It then creates a new user with password access and full privileges. The new user can now connect to the MySQL DBMS using the specified name and password:

SQL

sys-fcn.sql

```
# Get the version number and current user.
SELECT VERSION() , USER() ;

# Get the thread identity.
SHOW PROCESSLIST ;

# Create a new user with full privileges.
CREATE USER 'monty'@'localhost' IDENTIFIED BY 'monty-pwd' ;
GRANT ALL PRIVILEGES ON *.* TO 'monty'@'localhost' ;

# Confirm privileges for the new user.
SHOW GRANTS FOR monty@localhost ;
```

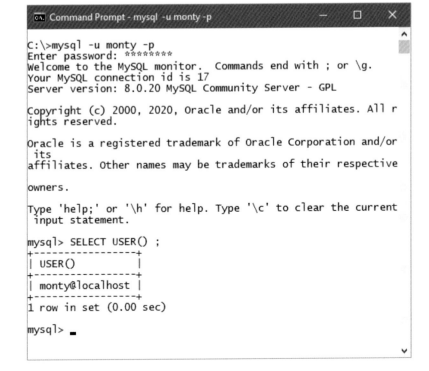

```
MySQL Command Line Client                          —    □    ✕

mysql> SOURCE C:\SQL\sys-fcn.sql
+-----------+----------------+
| VERSION() | USER()         |
+-----------+----------------+
| 8.0.20    | root@localhost |
+-----------+----------------+
1 row in set (0.00 sec)

+----+----------------+-----------------+------+---------+
| Id | User           | Host            | db   | Command |
+----+----------------+-----------------+------+---------+
|  4 | event_scheduler| localhost       | NULL | Daemon  |
| 15 | root           | localhost:52138 | NULL | Query   |
+----+----------------+-----------------+------+---------+
2 rows in set (0.00 sec)

Query OK, 0 rows affected (0.12 sec)

Query OK, 0 rows affected (0.17 sec)

| Grants for monty@localhost

| GRANT SELECT, INSERT, UPDATE, DELETE, CREATE, DROP, RELOAD,
 ROLE ON *.* TO `monty`@`localhost`
----------------------------+
2 rows in set (0.00 sec)

mysql> _
```

Hot tip

Each DBMS can set a wide range of specific privileges for a user – please refer to your DBMS documentation for full details.

131

```
Command Prompt - mysql -u monty -p              —    □    ✕

C:\>mysql -u monty -p
Enter password: ********
Welcome to the MySQL monitor.  Commands end with ; or \g.
Your MySQL connection id is 17
Server version: 8.0.20 MySQL Community Server - GPL

Copyright (c) 2000, 2020, Oracle and/or its affiliates. All r
ights reserved.

Oracle is a registered trademark of Oracle Corporation and/or
 its
affiliates. Other names may be trademarks of their respective

owners.

Type 'help;' or '\h' for help. Type '\c' to clear the current
 input statement.

mysql> SELECT USER() ;
+----------------+
| USER()         |
+----------------+
| monty@localhost |
+----------------+
1 row in set (0.00 sec)

mysql> _
```

Don't forget

MySQL automatically stores user passwords in encrypted form. The password has in fact been typed after the "Enter password:" prompt but it does not appear as text in the window for security purposes.

Summary

- A function is an SQL keyword, followed by parentheses, that performs a specific operation when it is called.

- Data can be specified as arguments in function parentheses.

- SQL function names and syntax vary from one DBMS to another.

- A section of a text string can be extracted with the **SUBSTRING()** function.

- Strings can be converted to uppercase with the **UPPER()** function or to lowercase with the **LOWER()** function.

- The **SOUNDEX()** function will return data that matches, or is similar to, a specified string.

- The **MOD()** function is useful to determine odd or even values.

- Floating-point values can be rounded up to the nearest integer with the **CEILING()** function or down with the **FLOOR()** function.

- The **RAND()** function returns a random number from 0 to 1.0.

- Individual components of a **DATE** data type can be returned by the **DAYOFMONTH()**, **MONTHNAME()**, and **YEAR()** functions.

- Individual components of a **TIME** data type can be returned with the **SECOND()**, **MINUTE()**, and **HOUR()** functions.

- The current date is returned by the **CURDATE()** function and the current time is returned by the **CURTIME()** function.

- A combined **DATETIME** is returned by the **NOW()** function.

- Threads can be seen with a **SHOW PROCESSLIST** statement, and individual threads can be terminated with the **KILL()** function.

- The **GRANT** statement is used to create new users by specifying their name, privileges, and password.

- A user's privileges level can be examined with a **SHOW GRANTS** statement.

(11) Grouping table data

This chapter demonstrates SQL aggregate functions to summarize table data and filter grouped data.

Finding summary values

SQL aggregate functions operate on multiple rows of a database table to perform a preordained calculation and then return a single value. The returned value is a summary of data within that column rather than an actual item of data.

The **AVG()** aggregate function returns a summarized average value of all the values within the column specified as its argument. It counts both the number of rows and the sum of their values, then divides the total value by the total number of rows.

The **MAX()** aggregate function returns the single highest value in the column specified as its argument. It compares the value on the first row to that on the second row, and discards the lower value. It then compares the retained value to that on the next row and again discards the lower value. The operation continues in this manner until the value on the final row has been compared – when the remaining retained value is the highest in that column. Similarly, the **MIN()** aggregate function returns the single lowest value in a column by discarding the higher value in each comparison.

In the following SQL script example, the average, maximum and minimum values are calculated for the "price" column:

Hot tip

Any rows of the column that contain a **NULL** value are totally ignored by the **AVG()** function.

avg-max-min.sql

```sql
# Use the "my_database" database.
USE my_database ;

# Create a table called "multimeters".
CREATE TABLE IF NOT EXISTS multimeters
(
  id        INT            AUTO_INCREMENT PRIMARY KEY ,
  model     CHAR( 10 )     NOT NULL ,
  price     DECIMAL( 4,2 ) NOT NULL
) ;

# Insert 3 records into the "multimeters" table.
INSERT INTO multimeters ( model , price )
  VALUES ( "Standard" , 11.75 ) ;
INSERT INTO multimeters ( model , price )
  VALUES ( "Super" , 19.50 ) ;
INSERT INTO multimeters ( model , price )
  VALUES ( "DeLuxe" , 24.99 ) ;
```

```
# Display all data in the "multimeters" table.
SELECT * FROM multimeters ;

# Get the average price.
SELECT AVG( price ) AS avg_price
FROM multimeters ;

# Get the maximum price and minimum price.
SELECT MAX( price ) AS max_price , MIN( price ) AS min_price
FROM multimeters ;

# Delete this sample table.
DROP TABLE IF EXISTS multimeters ;
```

Notice here how multiple aggregate function calls are made from a single **SELECT** statement.

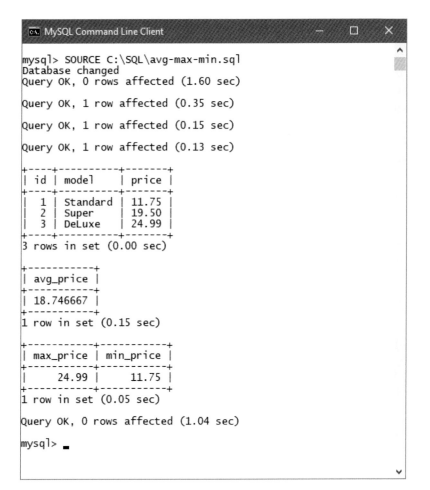

```
MySQL Command Line Client                    —    □    ×

mysql> SOURCE C:\SQL\avg-max-min.sql
Database changed
Query OK, 0 rows affected (1.60 sec)

Query OK, 1 row affected (0.35 sec)

Query OK, 1 row affected (0.15 sec)

Query OK, 1 row affected (0.13 sec)

+----+----------+-------+
| id | model    | price |
+----+----------+-------+
|  1 | Standard | 11.75 |
|  2 | Super    | 19.50 |
|  3 | DeLuxe   | 24.99 |
+----+----------+-------+
3 rows in set (0.00 sec)

+-----------+
| avg_price |
+-----------+
| 18.746667 |
+-----------+
1 row in set (0.15 sec)

+-----------+-----------+
| max_price | min_price |
+-----------+-----------+
|     24.99 |     11.75 |
+-----------+-----------+
1 row in set (0.05 sec)

Query OK, 0 rows affected (1.04 sec)

mysql> _
```

Some DBMSs, including MySQL, allow the **MIN()** and **MAX()** functions to be used on text values – **MAX()** returns the value that would be last if the values in that column were sorted alphabetically, and **MIN()** returns the value that would be first if the values in that column were sorted alphabetically.

Counting rows

The **COUNT()** aggregate function can determine the total number of rows in a database table. It can also count the number of rows in a specific column that do not contain a **NULL** value.

To return the total number of rows that a table contains, the * wildcard character must be specified as the function's argument:

```
COUNT ( * )
```

To return the number of non-empty rows in a particular column, the column's name must be specified as the function's argument:

```
COUNT ( column-name )
```

The SQL script example below creates a table populated with five records. Only two records have non-**NULL** values in the "email" column. The first call to the **COUNT()** function returns the total number of rows in this table. The second call to the **COUNT()** function returns just the number of rows where the "email" column does not contain a **NULL** value:

count.sql

```
# Use the "my_database" database.
USE my_database ;

# Create a table called "members".
CREATE TABLE IF NOT EXISTS members
(
  id        INT      AUTO_INCREMENT      PRIMARY KEY ,
  name      CHAR( 10 )       NOT NULL ,
  email     VARCHAR( 30 )
) ;

# Insert 5 records into the "members" table.
INSERT INTO members ( name )
  VALUES ( "Abraham" ) ;

INSERT INTO members ( name , email )
  VALUES( "Homer" , "homer@mailserver.usa" ) ;
```

```
INSERT INTO members ( name )
  VALUES ( "Marge" ) ;

INSERT INTO members ( name , email )
  VALUES( "Bart" , "bart@mailserver.usa" ) ;

INSERT INTO members ( name ) VALUES ( "Lisa" ) ;

# Count the total number of rows.
SELECT COUNT( * ) AS total_number_of_rows
FROM members ;

# Count the total number of rows.
SELECT COUNT( email ) AS rows_with_email_addresses
FROM members ;

# Delete this sample table.
DROP TABLE IF EXISTS members ;
```

Beware

Specifying the * wildcard character as the **COUNT()** argument returns the total number of rows including those containing **NULL** values – columns with **NULL** values are ignored, however, when a column name is specified as the **COUNT()** argument.

Discovering total values

The **SUM()** aggregate function returns the sum total of all values in the column specified as its argument. It can return the total of specific rows if the **SELECT** statement is qualified by a **WHERE** clause. It can also return the total of a calculated value by including an arithmetical expression within its parentheses.

In the following SQL script example, a table is populated with five records that contain order numbers and unit cost values. The first call to the **SUM()** function performs an addition that returns the total cost of all values from order number "10031". The second call to the **SUM()** function performs a multiplication that returns the total cost of values from order number "10030":

SQL

sum.sql

```
# Use the "my_database" database.
USE my_database ;

# Create a table called "star_orders".
CREATE TABLE IF NOT EXISTS star_orders
(
  id            INT           AUTO_INCREMENT          PRIMARY KEY ,
  order_num     INT                         NOT NULL ,
  cost_each     DECIMAL( 6,2 )  NOT NULL ,
  quantity      INT                         DEFAULT 1
) ;

# Insert 5 records into the "star_orders" table.
INSERT INTO star_orders ( order_num , cost_each , quantity )
  VALUES ( 10030 , 217.50, 2 ) ;
INSERT INTO star_orders ( order_num , cost_each )
  VALUES ( 10031 , 72.50 ) ;
INSERT INTO star_orders ( order_num , cost_each )
  VALUES ( 10032 , 299.75 ) ;
INSERT INTO star_orders ( order_num , cost_each )
  VALUES ( 10031 , 29.25 ) ;
INSERT INTO star_orders ( order_num , cost_each )
  VALUES ( 10031 , 148.25 ) ;

# Display all data in the "star_orders" table.
SELECT * FROM star_orders ;
```

Columns that contain a **NULL** value are ignored by the **SUM()** function.

```
# Get total cost for order number 10031.
SELECT SUM( cost_each ) AS total_for_order_10031
FROM star_orders WHERE order_num = 10031 ;
```

```
# Get total cost for order number 10030.
SELECT SUM( cost_each * quantity ) AS total_for_order_10030
FROM star_orders WHERE order_num = 10030 ;
```

```
# Delete this sample table.
DROP TABLE IF EXISTS star_orders ;
```

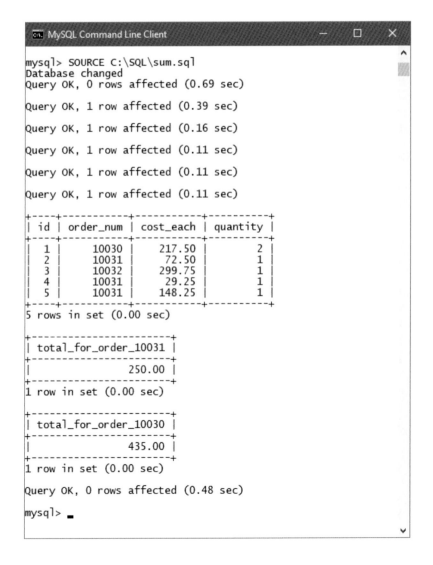

```
MySQL Command Line Client                          —    □    ×

mysql> SOURCE C:\SQL\sum.sql
Database changed
Query OK, 0 rows affected (0.69 sec)

Query OK, 1 row affected (0.39 sec)

Query OK, 1 row affected (0.16 sec)

Query OK, 1 row affected (0.11 sec)

Query OK, 1 row affected (0.11 sec)

Query OK, 1 row affected (0.11 sec)

+----+-----------+-----------+----------+
| id | order_num | cost_each | quantity |
+----+-----------+-----------+----------+
|  1 |     10030 |    217.50 |        2 |
|  2 |     10031 |     72.50 |        1 |
|  3 |     10032 |    299.75 |        1 |
|  4 |     10031 |     29.25 |        1 |
|  5 |     10031 |    148.25 |        1 |
+----+-----------+-----------+----------+
5 rows in set (0.00 sec)

+-----------------------+
| total_for_order_10031 |
+-----------------------+
|                250.00 |
+-----------------------+
1 row in set (0.00 sec)

+-----------------------+
| total_for_order_10030 |
+-----------------------+
|                435.00 |
+-----------------------+
1 row in set (0.00 sec)

Query OK, 0 rows affected (0.48 sec)

mysql> _
```

Hot tip

All the SQL aggregate functions – **SUM()**, **COUNT()**, **AVG()**, **MAX()**, and **MIN()** – can perform calculations on multiple column values, like the second call to the **SUM()** function in this example.

Working with distinct values

The **COUNT()** aggregate function can be forced to ignore a row that contains a value duplicating a value that has already appeared in a previously counted row. This is achieved by adding the **DISTINCT** keyword before the specified column name within the **COUNT()** function's parentheses.

Using the **DISTINCT** keyword ensures the **COUNT()** function will only count rows with unique values in the specified column.

The **DISTINCT** keyword can also be used to retrieve only unique text values from a column.

The example below demonstrates the effect on counting rows in a table both with and without the **DISTINCT** keyword. It also lists all the unique values from the "stone" column:

distinct.sql

```
# Use the "my_database" database.
USE my_database ;
```

```
# Create a table called "rings".
CREATE TABLE IF NOT EXISTS rings
(
  id        INT          AUTO_INCREMENT PRIMARY KEY ,
  stone     CHAR( 10 )   NOT NULL ,
  price     DECIMAL( 4,2 )  NOT NULL
) ;
```

```
# Insert 5 records into the "rings" table.
INSERT INTO rings ( stone , price ) VALUES ( "Ruby" , 40.00 ) ;
INSERT INTO rings ( stone , price ) VALUES( "Emerald" , 40.00 ) ;
INSERT INTO rings ( stone , price ) VALUES( "Diamond" , 60.00 ) ;
INSERT INTO rings ( stone , price ) VALUES( "Diamond" , 50.00 ) ;
INSERT INTO rings ( stone , price ) VALUES( "Garnet" , 40.00 ) ;
```

```
# Display all data in the "rings" table.
SELECT * FROM rings ;
```

```
# Get the total number of rows.
SELECT COUNT( price ) AS num_prices FROM rings ;
```

```
# Get the number of unique rows.
SELECT COUNT( DISTINCT price ) AS num_distinct_prices
FROM rings ;
```

The **DISTINCT** keyword cannot be used with the * wildcard character in the **COUNT()** function – a column name must be specified.

Get all the unique stone values.
SELECT DISTINCT stone **AS** unique_stone_names **FROM** rings ;

Delete this sample table.
DROP TABLE IF EXISTS rings ;

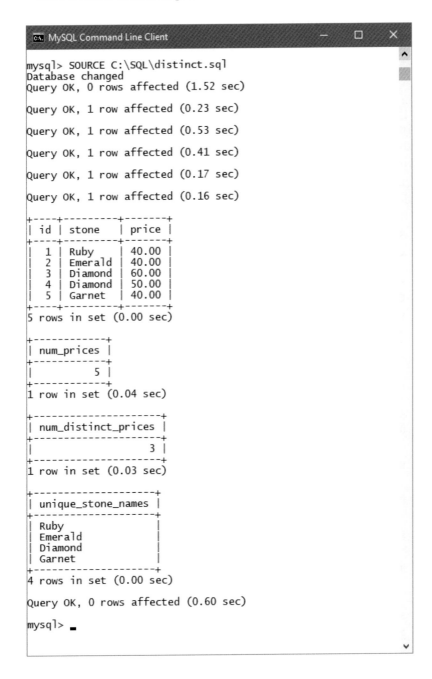

Hot tip

Some DBMSs allow the **DISTINCT** keyword to be used with other aggregate functions, such as **SUM()**.

Creating data groups

All previous examples in this chapter have used aggregate functions to perform a single operation on all the data in a column, or on data that matches a specified **WHERE** clause. This process can be refined by first arranging the data into logical groups so that the aggregate function operation can be performed on each group.

Data can be grouped by adding a **GROUP BY** clause to the end of a **SELECT** statement. This specifies a column name around which to arrange the groups. An aggregate function will then operate once on each group.

In this example, the data is first grouped around the "wood" column – the **COUNT()** function operates on each group to return the number of items in each type of wood. Next, the data is grouped around the "item" column – the **COUNT()** function returns the number of woods for each type of item:

by-group.sql

```
# Use the "my_database" database.
USE my_database ;

# Create a table called "cabinets".
CREATE TABLE IF NOT EXISTS cabinets
(
  id        INT     AUTO_INCREMENT      PRIMARY KEY ,
  wood      CHAR( 10 )    NOT NULL ,
  item      CHAR( 20 )    NOT NULL
) ;

# Insert 5 records into the "cabinets" table.
INSERT INTO cabinets ( wood , item )
  VALUES ( "Pine" , "Bookcase" ) ;
INSERT INTO cabinets ( wood , item )
  VALUES ( "Beech" , "Bookcase" ) ;
INSERT INTO cabinets ( wood , item )
  VALUES ( "Oak" , "Bookcase" ) ;
INSERT INTO cabinets ( wood , item )
  VALUES ( "Pine" , "Display Case" ) ;
INSERT INTO cabinets ( wood , item )
  VALUES ( "Oak" , "Display Case" ) ;

# Display all data in the "cabinets" table.
SELECT * FROM cabinets ;
```

...cont'd

```
# Get the number of items for each type of wood.
SELECT wood, COUNT( * ) AS num_items
FROM cabinets GROUP BY wood ;
```

```
# Get the number of woods for each type of item.
SELECT item, COUNT( * ) AS num_woods
FROM cabinets GROUP BY item ;
```

```
# Delete this sample table.
DROP TABLE IF EXISTS cabinets ;
```

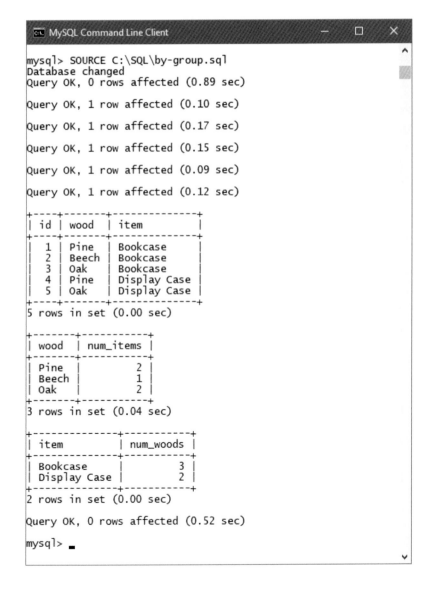

A **GROUP BY** clause must appear in the **SELECT** statement after any **WHERE** clause and before **ORDER BY** clause.

143

Filtering grouped data

Specific groups can be selected for inclusion in a **SELECT** statement in a similar way that specific rows can be selected using a **WHERE** clause. The **WHERE** clause works on rows of data but cannot be used to filter groups of data. Instead, the **HAVING** keyword is used to filter groups.

A **HAVING** clause is very similar to a **WHERE** clause – except that **WHERE** filters rows and **HAVING** filters groups.

Another distinction to make between these two clauses is that the **WHERE** clause filters before data is grouped, and the **HAVING** clause filters after data is grouped.

The following SQL script example filters out all items priced below 150.00 with a **WHERE** clause – this leaves 1 item each in the "Red" group and "Terracotta" group, and 2 items in the "Blue" group. It then filters out groups that contain just a single item with a **HAVING** clause – leaving just the "Blue" group:

having.sql

```
# Use the "my_database" database.
USE my_database ;

# Create a table called "sofabeds".
CREATE TABLE IF NOT EXISTS sofabeds
(
  id       INT        AUTO_INCREMENT        PRIMARY KEY ,
  name     CHAR( 10 )      NOT NULL ,
  color    CHAR( 10 )      NOT NULL ,
  price    DECIMAL( 6,2 )  NOT NULL
) ;

# Insert 5 records into the "sofabeds" table.
INSERT INTO sofabeds ( name , color, price )
  VALUES ( "Milan" , "Blue" , 199.99 ) ;
INSERT INTO sofabeds ( name , color , price )
  VALUES ( "Firenze" , "Red" , 144.99 ) ;
INSERT INTO sofabeds ( name , color , price )
  VALUES ( "Vivaldi" , "Terracotta" , 199.99 ) ;
INSERT INTO sofabeds ( name , color , price )
  VALUES ( "Vienna" , "Blue" , 164.99 ) ;
INSERT INTO sofabeds ( name , color , price )
  VALUES ( "Roma" , "Red" , 249.99 ) ;
```

```
# Display all data in the "sofabeds" table.
SELECT * FROM sofabeds ;

# Get the number of items for each color
# where the price exceeds 150.00 and
# when there is more than 1 item for that color.
SELECT color , COUNT( * ) AS num_items_over_150
FROM sofabeds
WHERE price >= 150.00
GROUP BY color
HAVING COUNT( * ) > 1 ;

# Delete this sample table.
DROP TABLE IF EXISTS sofabeds ;
```

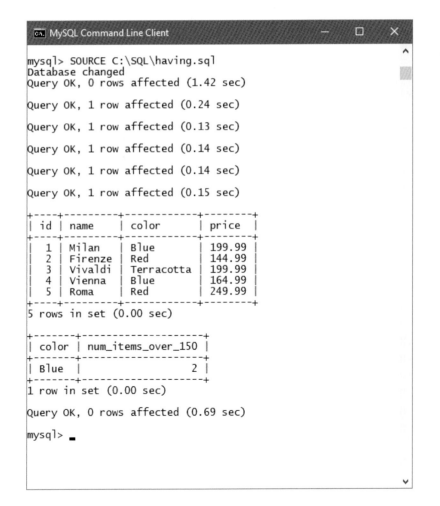

Don't forget

Only use a **HAVING** clause after a **GROUP BY** clause – use a **WHERE** clause to filter rows.

145

Sorting filtered group data

A **GROUP BY** clause cannot be relied upon to sort groups into order, but an **ORDER BY** clause can be added at the very end of a **SELECT** statement for this purpose.

It is important that multiple clauses in a **SELECT** statement appear in the correct order. The table below reviews the correct order:

Clause	Specifies
SELECT	Column/s or expressions to return
FROM	Table to retrieve data from
WHERE	Row-level filter
GROUP BY	Column to group around
HAVING	Group-level filter
ORDER BY	Return sort order

Each one of these clauses appears in the following example, which sorts the returned groups into numerical order:

sort-group.sql

```
USE my_database ;          # Use the "my_database" database.

# Create a table called "tub".
CREATE TABLE IF NOT EXISTS tub
(
    id          INT             AUTO_INCREMENT PRIMARY KEY ,
    num         INT             NOT NULL ,
    ref         VARCHAR( 10 )   NOT NULL ,
    qty         INT             DEFAULT 1,
    col         CHAR( 10 )      NOT NULL
) ;

# Insert 10 records into the "tub" table.
INSERT INTO tub ( num , ref , col ) VALUES ( 8004 , 101 , "Red" ) ;
INSERT INTO tub ( num , ref , col ) VALUES ( 8004 , 103 , "Lime" ) ;
INSERT INTO tub ( num , ref , col ) VALUES ( 8004 , 104 , "Blue" ) ;
INSERT INTO tub ( num , ref , col ) VALUES ( 8003 , 104 , "Blue" ) ;
INSERT INTO tub ( num , ref , col ) VALUES ( 8002 , 105 , "Red" ) ;
INSERT INTO tub ( num , ref , col ) VALUES ( 8002 , 102 , "Lime" ) ;
INSERT INTO tub ( num , ref , col ) VALUES ( 8002 , 103 , "Pink" ) ;
INSERT INTO tub ( num , ref , col ) VALUES ( 8001 , 104 , "Red" ) ;
INSERT INTO tub ( num , ref , col ) VALUES ( 8001 , 105 , "Lime" ) ;
INSERT INTO tub ( num , ref , col ) VALUES ( 8004 , 102 , "Blue" ) ;
```

```
# Display all data in the "tub" table.
SELECT * FROM tub ;

# Get the order number and number of items ordered
# where the color is not Pink
# and the number of items ordered is fewer than 3
# sorted by order number.
SELECT num , COUNT( * ) AS num_items
FROM tub WHERE col != "Pink"
GROUP BY num HAVING COUNT( * ) < 3 ORDER BY num ;

# Delete this sample table.
DROP TABLE IF EXISTS tub ;
```

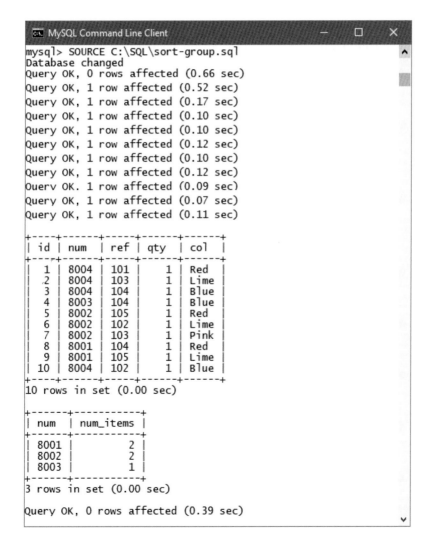

This example uses a variety of the techniques introduced in this chapter.

Summary

- Aggregate functions operate on multiple rows of a database table to perform a preordained calculation, then return a single value.

- The five standard aggregate functions in SQL are **AVG()**, **MAX()**, **MIN()**, **SUM()**, and **COUNT()**.

- Each aggregate function must state the column/s to operate on as the argument within its parentheses.

- The **AVG()** function returns the average of all the values in its specified column.

- **MAX()** returns the highest value of the data within its specified column and **MIN()** returns its lowest value.

- **SUM()** returns the sum total of all the values within the specified column.

- **COUNT()** can specify the * wildcard character as its argument in order to return the total number of rows in a table, or a column name to return the number of non-empty rows in that column.

- **NULL** data values are generally ignored by aggregate functions – except when the **COUNT()** function specifies the * wildcard character as its argument.

- The **DISTINCT** keyword ensures that only unique instances of a data value are operated upon.

- Data can be grouped with a **GROUP BY** clause to allow an aggregate function to operate on each group.

- A **WHERE** clause filters <u>rows</u> <u>before</u> data is grouped, and a **HAVING** clause filters <u>groups</u> <u>after</u> data is grouped.

- The **GROUP BY** clause does not ensure any sort order – an **ORDER BY** clause must be used to specify a sort order.

- The clauses in a **SELECT** statement must appear in the correct order – **SELECT, FROM, WHERE, GROUP BY, HAVING, ORDER BY**.

12 Making complex queries

This chapter demonstrates how a single query can address multiple tables, and how multiple queries can return a single results set.

Using sub-queries

Every **SELECT** statement is an SQL query. Many DBMSs allow a **SELECT** statement to be nested within another **SELECT** statement. The inner **SELECT** statement is known as a sub-query.

Sub-queries are useful to retrieve data from a table specifying what an outer **SELECT** statement should return from another table. For instance, imagine a table named "customers" containing name and account numbers, and another table named "orders" containing order numbers and customer account numbers. A query to identify the name of a customer who placed a particular order might look like this:

```
SELECT name FROM customers WHERE acc_num IN
  ( SELECT acc_num FROM orders WHERE ord_num = 4 ) ;
```

The inner sub-query is processed first. In this case, it returns the customer account number for order number 4 in the "orders" table. The outer query then matches the customer account number and returns the name of that customer.

Beware

Sub-queries are not supported in MySQL prior to version 4.1.

Notice that both tables have a column named "acc_num". This is perfectly acceptable – each column can be referenced explicitly using dot syntax as "customers.acc_num" and "orders.acc_num".

SELECT statements that contain sub-queries can be difficult to read and debug as they become more complex. There is, however, often an alternative to sub-queries. The following SQL script rewrites the example given above to provide the same functionality without using a sub-query:

SQL

subquery.sql

```
# Use the "my_database" database.
USE my_database ;

# Create a table called "customers".
CREATE TABLE IF NOT EXISTS customers
( acc_num INT PRIMARY KEY ,    name CHAR( 20 ) NOT NULL ) ;

# Insert 2 records into the "customers" table.
INSERT INTO customers ( acc_num , name )
  VALUES ( 123 , "T.Smith" ) ;
INSERT INTO customers ( acc_num , name )
  VALUES ( 124 , "P.Jones" ) ;
```

```
# Create a table called "orders".
CREATE TABLE IF NOT EXISTS orders
( ord_num INT PRIMARY KEY , acc_num INT NOT NULL ) ;

# Insert 2 records into the "orders" table.
INSERT INTO orders ( ord_num , acc_num ) VALUES ( 3 , 123 ) ;
INSERT INTO orders ( ord_num , acc_num ) VALUES ( 4 , 124 ) ;

# Display all data in "customers" and "orders" tables.
SELECT * FROM customers ; SELECT * FROM orders ;

# Retrieve the name of the customer placing order 4.
SELECT  ord_num , customers.acc_num , name
FROM customers , orders
WHERE customers.acc_num = orders.acc_num
AND orders.ord_num = 4 ;

# Delete these sample tables.
DROP TABLE IF EXISTS customers ;
DROP TABLE IF EXISTS orders ;
```

Hot tip

Always use the dot syntax to explicitly identify table columns wherever there is possible ambiguity.

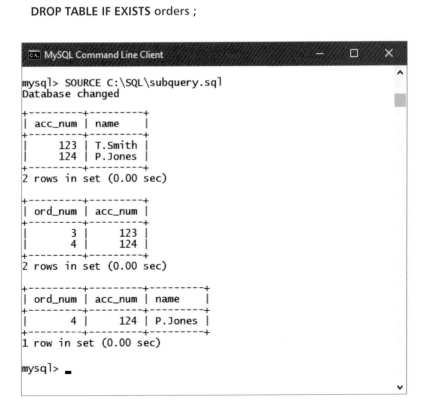

```
mysql> SOURCE C:\SQL\subquery.sql
Database changed

+---------+---------+
| acc_num | name    |
+---------+---------+
|     123 | T.Smith |
|     124 | P.Jones |
+---------+---------+
2 rows in set (0.00 sec)

+---------+---------+
| ord_num | acc_num |
+---------+---------+
|       3 |     123 |
|       4 |     124 |
+---------+---------+
2 rows in set (0.00 sec)

+---------+---------+---------+
| ord_num | acc_num | name    |
+---------+---------+---------+
|       4 |     124 | P.Jones |
+---------+---------+---------+
1 row in set (0.00 sec)

mysql> _
```

Don't forget

The usual "Query OK" confirmations have been removed from all further screenshots within this book in order to save space.

Sub-query calculated fields

A sub-query can be used to generate a calculated field that returns values from a table to an outer **SELECT** statement.

Given the "customers" and "orders" tables from the previous example on pages 150-151, a sub-query could use the **COUNT()** aggregate function to calculate how many orders have been placed by each account number in the "orders" table. The outer **SELECT** statement can then retrieve each customer name to display with this calculated field. The **SELECT** query and sub-query could look like this:

```
SELECT name ,
  ( SELECT COUNT( * ) FROM orders
    WHERE orders.acc_num = customers.acc_num )
  AS number_of_orders FROM customers
  ORDER BY customers.acc_num ;
```

The script below produces the same result without a sub-query. Both methods generate a "number_of_orders" calculated field alongside customer names, sorted by their account number:

subquery-calc.sql

```
# Use the "my_database" database.
USE my_database ;

# Create a table called "customers".
CREATE TABLE IF NOT EXISTS customers
( acc_num INT PRIMARY KEY ,    name CHAR( 20 ) NOT NULL ) ;

# Insert 3 records into the "customers" table.
INSERT INTO customers ( acc_num , name )
  VALUES ( 123 , "T.Smith" ) ;
INSERT INTO customers ( acc_num , name )
  VALUES ( 124 , "P.Jones" ) ;
INSERT INTO customers ( acc_num , name )
  VALUES ( 125 , "H.Nicks" ) ;

# Create a table called "orders".
CREATE TABLE IF NOT EXISTS orders
( ord_num INT PRIMARY KEY , acc_num INT NOT NULL ) ;

# Insert 5 records into the "orders" table.
INSERT INTO orders ( ord_num , acc_num ) VALUES ( 1 , 123 ) ;
INSERT INTO orders ( ord_num , acc_num ) VALUES ( 2 , 124 ) ;
```

```
INSERT INTO orders ( ord_num , acc_num ) VALUES ( 3 , 125 ) ;
INSERT INTO orders ( ord_num , acc_num ) VALUES ( 4 , 125 ) ;
INSERT INTO orders ( ord_num , acc_num ) VALUES ( 5 , 123 ) ;

# Display all data in "customers" and "orders" tables.
SELECT * FROM customers ; SELECT * FROM orders ;

# Get the number of orders per customer.
SELECT name , customers.acc_num , COUNT( * )
AS number_of_orders
FROM  customers , orders
WHERE customers.acc_num = orders.acc_num
GROUP BY name ORDER BY customers.acc_num ;

# Delete these sample tables.
DROP TABLE IF EXISTS customers ;
DROP TABLE IF EXISTS orders ;
```

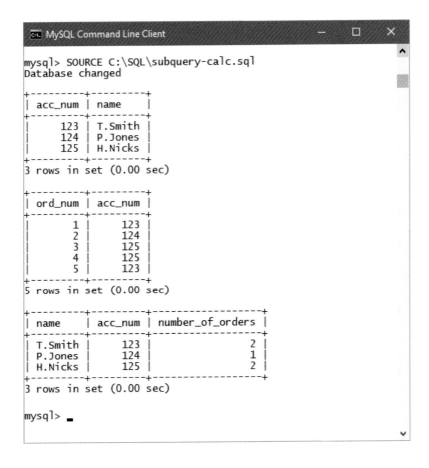

```
mysql> SOURCE C:\SQL\subquery-calc.sql
Database changed

+---------+---------+
| acc_num | name    |
+---------+---------+
|     123 | T.Smith |
|     124 | P.Jones |
|     125 | H.Nicks |
+---------+---------+
3 rows in set (0.00 sec)

+---------+---------+
| ord_num | acc_num |
+---------+---------+
|       1 |     123 |
|       2 |     124 |
|       3 |     125 |
|       4 |     125 |
|       5 |     123 |
+---------+---------+
5 rows in set (0.00 sec)

+---------+---------+------------------+
| name    | acc_num | number_of_orders |
+---------+---------+------------------+
| T.Smith |     123 |                2 |
| P.Jones |     124 |                1 |
| H.Nicks |     125 |                2 |
+---------+---------+------------------+
3 rows in set (0.00 sec)

mysql> _
```

Combining queries

Multiple **SELECT** queries can be made to combine their returns into a single "result set" using the **UNION** keyword. The **SELECT** statements may query the same table, or different tables, but each statement must have the same format:

- Each query must specify the same column names, expressions, and aggregate function calls.

- Specified column names, expressions, and function calls must appear in precisely the same order in each query.

- Column data types must be compatible – they need not be identical, but of similar types that can be converted.
  For instance, similar numeric types or similar date types.

There are no standard limits to the number of **SELECT** queries that can be combined with the **UNION** keyword. The following example combines the returns from three **SELECT** queries, made to three different tables, into a single common result set:

union.sql

```
# Use the "my_database" database.
USE my_database ;

# Create a table called "ps_games".
CREATE TABLE IF NOT EXISTS ps_games
( code VARCHAR( 10 ) , title CHAR( 20 ) , ages VARCHAR( 3 ) ) ;

# Insert 2 records into the "ps_games" table.
INSERT INTO ps_games ( code , title , ages )
  VALUES ( "567/3573" , "Crash Bash Platinum" , "3+" ) ;
INSERT INTO ps_games ( code , title , ages )
  VALUES ( "567/0301" , "The Italian Job" , "11+" ) ;

# Create a table called "xbox_games".
CREATE TABLE IF NOT EXISTS xbox_games
( code VARCHAR( 10 ) , title CHAR( 20 ) , ages VARCHAR( 3 ) ) ;

# Insert 2 records into the "xbox_games" table.
INSERT INTO xbox_games ( code , title , ages )
  VALUES ( "567/2660" , "Blinx" , "3+" ) ;
INSERT INTO xbox_games ( code , title , ages )
  VALUES ( "567/0569" , "Turok Evolution" , "15+" ) ;
```

```
# Create a table called "cube_games".
CREATE TABLE IF NOT EXISTS cube_games
( code VARCHAR( 10 ) , title CHAR( 20 ) , ages VARCHAR( 3 ) ) ;

# Insert 2 records into the "cube_games" table.
INSERT INTO cube_games ( code , title , ages )
  VALUES ( "567/0428" , "Scooby-Doo" , "3+" ) ;
INSERT INTO cube_games ( code , title , ages )
  VALUES ( "567/0411" , "Resident Evil" , "15+" ) ;

# Display all data in "ps_games", "xbox_games"
# and "cube_games" as a single result set.
SELECT * FROM ps_games
UNION
SELECT * FROM xbox_games
UNION
SELECT * FROM cube_games ;

# Delete these sample tables.
DROP TABLE IF EXISTS ps_games ;
DROP TABLE IF EXISTS xbox_games ;
DROP TABLE IF EXISTS cube_games ;
```

Don't forget

The data within the tables is not actually affected – the **UNION** only determines how the returns are presented.

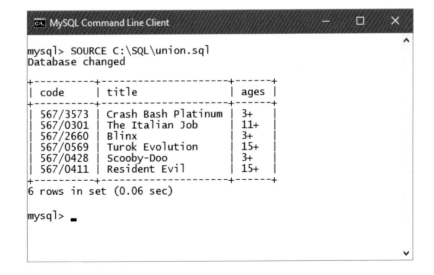

```
mysql> SOURCE C:\SQL\union.sql
Database changed

+-----------+----------------------+-------+
| code      | title                | ages  |
+-----------+----------------------+-------+
| 567/3573  | Crash Bash Platinum  | 3+    |
| 567/0301  | The Italian Job      | 11+   |
| 567/2660  | Blinx                | 3+    |
| 567/0569  | Turok Evolution      | 15+   |
| 567/0428  | Scooby-Doo           | 3+    |
| 567/0411  | Resident Evil        | 15+   |
+-----------+----------------------+-------+
6 rows in set (0.06 sec)

mysql> _
```

Hot tip

Refer to your DBMS documentation to check that it does not impose a maximum statement restriction.

Handling duplicate rows

The default behavior of the **UNION** keyword automatically excludes any duplicate rows from the data returned by the **SELECT** statement.

It is sometimes preferable to have the **SELECT** statement return all rows, including duplicates, by using a **UNION ALL** clause rather than just the **UNION** keyword.

In this example, the SQL script creates two tables, each populated with two records – the second rows in each table are identical. The **SELECT** query using the **UNION** keyword only returns one instance of that data, whereas the **SELECT** query using the **UNION ALL** clause returns both instances:

union-all.sql

```
# Use the "my_database" database.
USE my_database ;

# Create a table called "ps_games" & insert 2 records.
CREATE TABLE IF NOT EXISTS ps_games
( title CHAR( 20 ) , ages VARCHAR( 3 ) ) ;
INSERT INTO ps_games ( title , ages )
  VALUES ( "Grand Theft Auto" , "18+" ) ;
INSERT INTO ps_games ( title , ages )
  VALUES ( "Colin McRae Rally" , "11+" ) ;

# Create a table called "xbox_games" & insert 2 records.
CREATE TABLE IF NOT EXISTS xbox_games
( title CHAR( 20 ) , ages VARCHAR( 3 ) ) ;
INSERT INTO xbox_games ( title , ages )
  VALUES ( "Splinter Cell" , "15+" ) ;
INSERT INTO xbox_games ( title , ages )
  VALUES ( "Colin McRae Rally" , "11+" ) ;

# Display all data in the "ps_games" and "xbox_games".
SELECT * FROM ps_games ;
SELECT * FROM xbox_games ;

# Display unique data in "ps_games" and "xbox_games".
SELECT * FROM ps_games
UNION
SELECT * FROM xbox_games ;
```

Display all data in "ps_games" and "xbox_games".
SELECT * FROM ps_games
UNION ALL
SELECT * FROM xbox_games ;

Delete these sample tables.
DROP TABLE IF EXISTS ps_games ;
DROP TABLE IF EXISTS xbox_games ;

```
MySQL Command Line Client                    —    □    ×

mysql> SOURCE C:\SQL\union-all.sql
Database changed

+--------------------+------+
| title              | ages |
+--------------------+------+
| Grand Theft Auto   | 18+  |
| Colin McRae Rally  | 11+  |
+--------------------+------+
2 rows in set (0.00 sec)

+--------------------+------+
| title              | ages |
+--------------------+------+
| Splinter Cell      | 15+  |
| Colin McRae Rally  | 11+  |
+--------------------+------+
2 rows in set (0.00 sec)

+--------------------+------+
| title              | ages |
+--------------------+------+
| Grand Theft Auto   | 18+  |
| Colin McRae Rally  | 11+  |
| Splinter Cell      | 15+  |
+--------------------+------+
3 rows in set (0.01 sec)

+--------------------+------+
| title              | ages |
+--------------------+------+
| Grand Theft Auto   | 18+  |
| Colin McRae Rally  | 11+  |
| Splinter Cell      | 15+  |
| Colin McRae Rally  | 11+  |
+--------------------+------+
4 rows in set (0.00 sec)

mysql> _
```

Sorting combined results

The data returned from multiple tables using the **UNION** keyword can be sorted into a specified order by adding a single **ORDER BY** clause after the final **SELECT** statement. It may appear to apply only to that final **SELECT** statement, but will, in fact, sort the data returned from all the **SELECT** statements.

In the following SQL script example, data returned from two tables is combined and sorted into order – first numerically, then alphabetically:

union-sort.sql

```
# Use the "my_database" database.
USE my_database ;

# Create a table called "hers" and insert 3 records.
CREATE TABLE IF NOT EXISTS hers
( id INT AUTO_INCREMENT PRIMARY KEY , name CHAR( 20 ) ) ;
INSERT INTO hers ( name ) VALUES ( "Linda" ) ;
INSERT INTO hers ( name ) VALUES ( "Donna" ) ;
INSERT INTO hers ( name ) VALUES ( "Kay" ) ;

# Create a table called "his" and insert 3 records.
CREATE TABLE IF NOT EXISTS his
( id INT AUTO_INCREMENT PRIMARY KEY , name CHAR( 20 ) ) ;
INSERT INTO his ( name ) VALUES ( "Michael" ) ;
INSERT INTO his ( name ) VALUES ( "David" ) ;
INSERT INTO his ( name ) VALUES ( "Andrew" ) ;

# Display all data in the "hers" and "his" table.
SELECT * FROM hers ;
SELECT * FROM his ;

# Display all data in "hers" and "his" sorted by id.
SELECT * FROM hers
UNION
SELECT * FROM his ORDER BY id ;

# Display all data in "hers" and "his" sorted by name.
SELECT * FROM hers
UNION
SELECT * FROM his ORDER BY name ;

# Delete these sample tables.
DROP TABLE IF EXISTS hers ;
DROP TABLE IF EXISTS his ;
```

```
MySQL Command Line Client                          —    □    ×

mysql> SOURCE C:\SQL\union-sort.sql
Database changed
+----+-------+
| id | name  |
+----+-------+
|  1 | Linda |
|  2 | Donna |
|  3 | Kay   |
+----+-------+
3 rows in set (0.00 sec)

+----+---------+
| id | name    |
+----+---------+
|  1 | Michael |
|  2 | David   |
|  3 | Andrew  |
+----+---------+
3 rows in set (0.00 sec)

+----+---------+
| id | name    |
+----+---------+
|  1 | Linda   |
|  1 | Michael |
|  2 | Donna   |
|  2 | David   |
|  3 | Kay     |
|  3 | Andrew  |
+----+---------+
6 rows in set (0.00 sec)

+----+---------+
| id | name    |
+----+---------+
|  3 | Andrew  |
|  2 | David   |
|  2 | Donna   |
|  3 | Kay     |
|  1 | Linda   |
|  1 | Michael |
+----+---------+
6 rows in set (0.00 sec)

mysql> _
```

Summary

- A **SELECT** query nested within another **SELECT** query is known as a "sub-query".

- An inner **SELECT** sub-query is always processed before the outer **SELECT** query in which it is nested.

- Sub-queries can retrieve data from a table to specify what an outer **SELECT** statement should return from another table.

- Columns, in tables containing columns with identical names, can be explicitly addressed using dot syntax, as table.column-name.

- Like regular **SELECT** statements, sub-queries can also generate calculated fields.

- **SELECT** statements containing sub-queries can be difficult to read and debug – there is often an alternative way to make the queries.

- The data returned from multiple **SELECT** queries can be combined into a single "result set" using the **UNION** keyword.

- All **SELECT** queries combined with the **UNION** keyword must have the same format for their columns and expressions.

- Data returned from multiple tables with the **UNION** keyword automatically excludes any duplicate rows.

- The **UNION ALL** clause ensures that each instance of duplicated rows is included in the returned data.

- Data returned from multiple tables using the **UNION** keyword can be sorted into a specified order by adding a single **ORDER BY** clause after the final **SELECT** statement.

13 Joining database tables

This chapter demonstrates the important topic of "joins" and explains why they are of such significance in SQL.

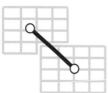

What are joins?

The ability to dynamically join together multiple tables with a single **SELECT** query is one of SQL's most powerful features. This allows related data to be efficiently stored in numerous tables, rather than in just one large table.

Storing data in numerous related tables is the essence of relational database design, and provides some important benefits. It is necessary to understand relational tables to fully appreciate the significance afforded by the join capability.

For instance, imagine a table containing a product catalog. This could typically have columns for catalog number, product name, and product price, together with the name and address of the vendor supplying each product. A table of this format containing data on various game products might look like this:

```
+----------+----------+-------+----------------+---------------------+
| id       | game     | price | vendor         | location            |
+----------+----------+-------+----------------+---------------------+
| 371/2209 | Scrabble | 14.50 | Mattel Inc     | El Segundo, CA, USA |
| 373/2296 | Jenga    |  6.99 | Hasbro Inc     | Pawtucket, RI, USA  |
| 360/9659 | Uno      | 11.99 | Mattel Inc     | El Segundo, CA, USA |
| 373/5372 | Connect  |  5.99 | J.W.Spear Plc  | Enfield, Middx, UK  |
| 370/9470 | Bingo    |  8.99 | J.W.Spear Plc  | Enfield, Middx, UK  |
+----------+----------+-------+----------------+---------------------+
```

Notice how the vendor data is laboriously repeated for catalog items that are created by the same vendor. This is undesirable, especially with a larger catalog, for these main reasons:

- It is an inefficient use of time to repeatedly input the same vendor data for each record.
- The database table size requires more space to store the repeated data.
- Each instance of the vendor data would need to be individually updated if their information changes – for example, if the vendor relocates to a new address.
- There is a possibility that the vendor data might not be input in the exact same format in every record – so creating inconsistent data that may produce misleading returns from SQL queries.

It is far more preferable to store the vendor data in a separate table and relate the vendor to the product by an identity reference. In the case of the games products, the previous table data could now appear in two separate tables, like this:

```
+---------+--------+----------+-------+
| id      | vendor | name     | price |
+---------+--------+----------+-------+
| 371/2209 |      1 | Scrabble | 14.50 |
| 373/2296 |      2 | Jenga    |  6.99 |
| 360/9659 |      1 | Uno      | 11.99 |
| 373/5372 |      3 | Connect  |  5.99 |
| 370/9470 |      3 | Bingo    |  8.99 |
+---------+--------+----------+-------+
```

```
+----+---------------+---------------------+
| id | name          | location            |
+----+---------------+---------------------+
|  1 | Mattel Inc    | El Segundo, CA, USA |
|  2 | Hasbro Inc    | Pawtucket, RI, USA  |
|  3 | J.W.Spear Plc | Enfield, Middx, UK  |
+----+---------------+---------------------+
```

Whenever a table column contains duplicate data, consider creating a separate table for that data.

These two compact tables store precisely the same information as the previous large table, and have these benefits:

- Duplicated vendor data need not be repeatedly entered.
- The database tables size requires less space.
- A single change is required should the vendor information need to be updated.
- The vendor data is assured to be consistent.

These tables are both created with the "id" column specified as the **PRIMARY KEY** to ensure that data in that column is unique in each row – so no product code can be duplicated and no vendor information can be duplicated.

Remember that like-named columns can be explicitly addressed using the dot syntax, such as "vendors.id" and "games.id".

The data in both tables can be retrieved using a single **SELECT** query to join the product data to the associated vendor data.

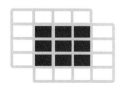

Creating a join

The data can be returned from multiple joined tables by stating the table names separated by a **JOIN** keyword, in the **FROM** clause of a **SELECT** statement.

A **WHERE** clause <u>must</u> then be added to the **SELECT** statement to define the relationship between data in each table. This acts as a filter to return only the data that satisfies the specified condition.

The following SQL script example creates the "games" and "vendors" tables shown on page 163. The **WHERE** clause in a **SELECT** query defines the relationship between data in the "vendor" column of the "games" table and the "id" column of the "vendors" table.

The **SELECT** column retrieves specific correctly-associated rows from these joined tables, listed under descriptive alias headings:

join.sql

```
# Use the "my_database" database.
USE my_database ;

# Create a table called "games".
CREATE TABLE IF NOT EXISTS games
(
   id          VARCHAR( 10 )   PRIMARY KEY ,
   vendor      INT             NOT NULL ,
   name        CHAR( 20 )      NOT NULL ,
   price       DECIMAL( 6,2 )  NOT NULL
) ;

# Insert 5 records into the "games" table.
INSERT INTO games ( id , vendor , name , price )
   VALUES ( "371/2209" , 1 , "Scrabble" , 14.50 ) ;
INSERT INTO games ( id , vendor , name , price )
   VALUES ( "373/2296" , 2 , "Jenga" , 6.99 ) ;
INSERT INTO games ( id , vendor , name , price )
   VALUES ( "360/9659" , 1 , "Uno" , 11.99 ) ;
INSERT INTO games ( id , vendor , name , price )
   VALUES ( "373/5372" , 3 , "Connect" , 5.99 ) ;
INSERT INTO games ( id , vendor , name , price )
   VALUES ( "370/9470" , 3 , "Bingo" , 8.99 ) ;
```

The join does not directly affect the table data itself – it simply extracts the required data dynamically.

```
# Create a table called "vendors".
CREATE TABLE IF NOT EXISTS vendors
(
  id          INT           PRIMARY KEY ,
  name        CHAR( 20 )    NOT NULL ,
  location    CHAR( 20 )    NOT NULL
) ;

# Insert 3 records into the "vendors" table.
INSERT INTO vendors ( id , name , location )
  VALUES ( 1 , "Mattel Inc" , "El Segundo, Ca, USA" ) ;
INSERT INTO vendors ( id , name , location )
  VALUES ( 2 , "Hasbro Inc" , "Pawtucket, RI, USA" ) ;
INSERT INTO vendors ( id , name , location )
  VALUES ( 3 , "J.W.Spear Plc" , "Enfield, Middx, UK" ) ;

# Display game code, name, price and vendor name
# for each game in the two joined tables.
SELECT      games.id        AS ProductCode ,
            games.name      AS Game ,
            vendors.name    AS Vendor ,
            games.price     AS Price
FROM        games JOIN vendors
WHERE       vendors.id = games.vendor ;

# Delete these sample tables.
DROP TABLE games ;
DROP TABLE vendors ;
```

Omission of the **WHERE** clause will return every row in the first table paired with every row in the second table – 15 rows in this case. This is not the desired result as no association has been made between data in each table.

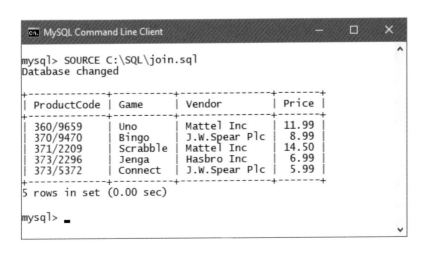

```
mysql> SOURCE C:\SQL\join.sql
Database changed

+-------------+----------+---------------+-------+
| ProductCode | Game     | Vendor        | Price |
+-------------+----------+---------------+-------+
| 360/9659    | Uno      | Mattel Inc    | 11.99 |
| 370/9470    | Bingo    | J.W.Spear Plc |  8.99 |
| 371/2209    | Scrabble | Mattel Inc    | 14.50 |
| 373/2296    | Jenga    | Hasbro Inc    |  6.99 |
| 373/5372    | Connect  | J.W.Spear Plc |  5.99 |
+-------------+----------+---------------+-------+
5 rows in set (0.00 sec)

mysql>
```

You may also see a join created using **INNER JOIN** keywords. An inner join is the default type of join, and the **INNER** keyword is optional, so it may be omitted. An inner join returns records that have matching values in both tables.

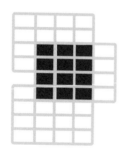

Joining multiple tables

There is theoretically no limit to the number of tables that can be joined by a single **SELECT** statement and the **JOIN** keyword. The length of time taken to process the query will, however, increase in proportion to the number of tables joined, and their sizes.

When joining multiple tables, the relationship between data in the first two tables must be defined in a **WHERE** clause, as with the previous example. The relationship of subsequent tables can then be defined using the **AND** keyword.

This example first defines the relationship between the "vendors" table and the "items" table, then that between the "items" table and the "orders" table. This allows data for a specific order to be retrieved with correctly-associated item and vendor information:

multi-join.sql

```
# Use the "my_database" database.
USE my_database ;

# Create a table called "items" with 3 records.
CREATE TABLE IF NOT EXISTS items
(
  id          INT            PRIMARY KEY ,
  vendor      INT            NOT NULL ,
  name        CHAR( 20 )     NOT NULL ,
  price       DECIMAL( 6,2 ) NOT NULL
) ;

INSERT INTO items ( id , vendor , name , price )
  VALUES ( 601 , 2 , "Elephants" , 147.50 ) ;
INSERT INTO items ( id , vendor , name , price )
  VALUES ( 602 , 2 , "Reindeer" , 123.00 ) ;
INSERT INTO items ( id , vendor , name , price )
  VALUES ( 603 , 1 , "Alligators" , 185.00 ) ;

# Create a table called "vendors" with 2 records.
CREATE TABLE IF NOT EXISTS vendors
(
  id          INT            PRIMARY KEY ,
  name        CHAR( 20 )     NOT NULL
) ;
INSERT INTO vendors ( id , name ) VALUES ( 1 , "Alpha Inc" ) ;
INSERT INTO vendors ( id , name ) VALUES ( 2 , "Zeta Inc" ) ;
```

```
# Create a table called "orders" with 3 records.
CREATE TABLE IF NOT EXISTS orders
(
  num        INT     PRIMARY KEY ,
  item       INT     NOT NULL ,
  qty        INT     NOT NULL
) ;
INSERT INTO orders ( num , item , qty )
  VALUES ( 2805 , 603 , 10 ) ;
INSERT INTO orders ( num , item , qty )
  VALUES ( 2806 , 603 , 5 ) ;
INSERT INTO orders ( num , item , qty )
  VALUES ( 2807 , 601 , 10 ) ;

# Display order number, quantity, item name, vendor
# and total order value of order number 2805.
SELECT          orders.num                 AS Number ,
                orders.qty                 AS Qty ,
                items.name                 AS Toy ,
                vendors.name               AS Vendor ,
                items.price * orders.qty   AS Total
FROM            items JOIN vendors JOIN orders
WHERE           vendors.id = items.vendor
AND             items.id = orders.item
AND             orders.num = 2805 ;

# Delete these sample tables.
DROP TABLE IF EXISTS items ;
DROP TABLE IF EXISTS vendors ;
DROP TABLE IF EXISTS orders ;
```

Hot tip

This **SELECT** statement specifies an alias name for each of the columns it queries with the **AS** keyword – some DBMSs, such as Oracle, do not require the **AS** keyword before the alias name.

167

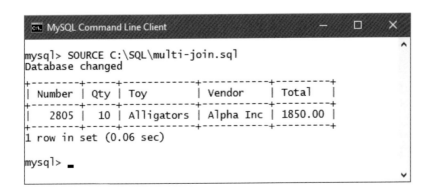

```
mysql> SOURCE C:\SQL\multi-join.sql
Database changed
+--------+-----+-----------+-----------+---------+
| Number | Qty | Toy       | Vendor    | Total   |
+--------+-----+-----------+-----------+---------+
|   2805 |  10 | Alligators | Alpha Inc | 1850.00 |
+--------+-----+-----------+-----------+---------+
1 row in set (0.06 sec)

mysql>
```

Creating self joins

The table joins demonstrated in the previous examples in this chapter are known as "equi-joins" because the relationship between the tables is defined by a test of equality. This type of join is also referred to as an "inner" join.

The rest of this chapter examines four other types of join: the "self join"; the "natural join"; the "left join"; and the "right join".

A self join enables a **SELECT** query to make more than one reference to the same table. In order to avoid ambiguity it must specify different alias names for the table using the **AS** keyword in the **FROM** clause. It can then explicitly address columns from each table using dot syntax.

The usefulness of a self join may not be immediately apparent without a practical example. Imagine a table containing personnel data, listing the name of each individual and the department where they are employed. A **SELECT** query could use a self join to return the name of all personnel in the department of any specified individual.

This example stores the personnel data in a table called "staff". In the **SELECT** statement this table is given two alias names of "s1" and "s2". Consider these to be two virtual tables containing identical data in identical columns.

The **WHERE** clause explicitly compares column data in the first virtual table with that in the second virtual table to discover the department in which the specified individual is employed. It then returns the name and department for all staff members in that department:

Hot tip

In many DBMSs self joins are processed faster than sub-queries.

self-join.sql

```
# Use the "my_database" database.
USE my_database ;

# Create a table called "staff".
CREATE TABLE IF NOT EXISTS staff
( dept CHAR( 20 ) NOT NULL , name CHAR( 20 ) PRIMARY KEY ) ;

# Insert 6 records into the "staff" table.
INSERT INTO staff ( dept , name )
  VALUES ( "Sales" , "Jo Brown" ) ;
INSERT INTO staff ( dept , name )
  VALUES ( "Legal" , "Max Tiler" ) ;
```

```
INSERT INTO staff ( dept , name )
  VALUES ( "Works" , "Ed Frost" ) ;
INSERT INTO staff ( dept , name )
  VALUES ( "Sales" , "Sue Ebner" ) ;
INSERT INTO staff ( dept , name )
  VALUES ( "Works" , "Al Morris" ) ;
INSERT INTO staff ( dept , name )
  VALUES ( "Sales" , "Tony West" ) ;

# Display all data in the "staff" table.
SELECT * FROM staff ;

# Display the all members of staff
# in the same department as Tony West.
SELECT  s1.dept AS Department , s1.name AS Name
FROM    staff AS s1 JOIN staff AS s2
WHERE   s1.dept = s2.dept AND s2.name = "Tony West" ;

# Delete this sample table.
DROP TABLE IF EXISTS staff ;
```

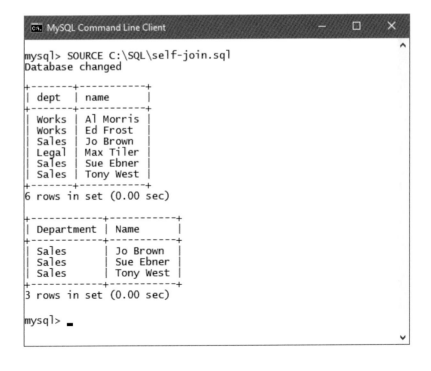

Notice that explicit addressing appears in the first part of this **SELECT** statement – even before the alias names have been specified in the **WHERE** clause. Always use explicit addressing with self joins to avoid ambiguity.

169

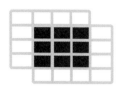

Creating natural joins

All table joins have at least one column that will also appear in another table – allowing the relationship between those tables to be defined. A natural join is simply a technique to eliminate a column that contains duplicate data.

Typically, the "*" wildcard character is used to return all the columns from the first table. Then specific, non-duplicating columns are joined from other tables. This is not a radical departure from previous examples, but merely offers alternative syntax rather than specifying each required column individually.

The following SQL script example creates and populates two database tables. Each table contains a column listing common part numbers that can be used to define the relationship between these two tables.

The **SELECT** query creates aliases for both tables. It then returns all the columns from the "parts" table, using the "p" alias with the "*" wildcard character, and the "price" column from the "parts_prices" table, using the "pp" alias with dot syntax.

natural-join.sql

```
# Use the "my_database" database.
USE my_database ;

# Create a table called "parts".
CREATE TABLE IF NOT EXISTS parts
( num INT PRIMARY KEY , name CHAR( 20 ) NOT NULL ) ;

# Insert 3 records into the "parts" table.
INSERT INTO parts ( num , name )
  VALUES ( 382131 , "Standard bracket" ) ;
INSERT INTO parts ( num , name )
  VALUES ( 382132 , "Slide bracket" ) ;
INSERT INTO parts ( num , name )
  VALUES ( 382133 , "Low-mount bracket" ) ;

# Create a table called "parts_prices".
CREATE TABLE IF NOT EXISTS parts_prices
(
  num  INT            PRIMARY KEY ,
  price DECIMAL( 6,2 )  NOT NULL
) ;
```

...cont'd

```
# Insert 3 records into the "parts_prices" table.
INSERT INTO parts_prices ( num , price )
  VALUES ( 382131 , 8.99 ) ;
INSERT INTO parts_prices ( num , price )
  VALUES ( 382132 , 10.99 ) ;
INSERT INTO parts_prices ( num , price )
  VALUES ( 382133 , 29.99 ) ;

# Display all data in "parts" and "parts_prices" tables.
SELECT * FROM parts ; SELECT * FROM parts_prices ;

# Display each part number, name and price.
SELECT          p.* , pp.price
FROM            parts AS p JOIN parts_prices AS pp
WHERE           p.num = pp.num ;

# Delete these sample tables.
DROP TABLE IF EXISTS parts ;
DROP TABLE IF EXISTS parts_prices ;
```

Hot tip

Table aliases are useful to shorten the SQL code – especially in more complex **SELECT** statements.

```
MySQL Command Line Client                        —    □    ×

mysql> SOURCE C:\SQL\natural-join.sql
Database changed

+--------+------------------+
| num    | name             |
+--------+------------------+
| 382131 | Standard bracket |
| 382132 | Slide bracket    |
| 382133 | Low-mount bracket |
+--------+------------------+
3 rows in set (0.00 sec)

+--------+-------+
| num    | price |
+--------+-------+
| 382131 |  8.99 |
| 382132 | 10.99 |
| 382133 | 29.99 |
+--------+-------+
3 rows in set (0.01 sec)

+--------+------------------+-------+
| num    | name             | price |
+--------+------------------+-------+
| 382131 | Standard bracket |  8.99 |
| 382132 | Slide bracket    | 10.99 |
| 382133 | Low-mount bracket | 29.99 |
+--------+------------------+-------+
3 rows in set (0.00 sec)

mysql> _
```

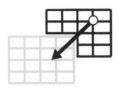

Specifying join direction

Mostly, table joins will be the standard inner, equi-join type that returns the data from rows where the column data matches for the defined relationship. Sometimes, however, it is desirable to also return data from rows that have no matched relationship. For instance, to include products with zero orders in a list of products and ordered quantities.

This can be achieved by adding the **JOIN** keyword to a **FROM** clause, preceded by the **LEFT** or **RIGHT** keyword.

When **LEFT JOIN** is specified, all the rows in the table specified to the left of this statement are joined to the table on its right. Conversely, when **RIGHT JOIN** is specified, all the rows in the table specified to the right of this statement are joined to the table on its left. In each case, the conditional test is now stated after the **ON** keyword, not in a **WHERE** clause.

This example demonstrates **JOIN** in both directions, to return data from rows that would normally be ignored by a standard inner join:

left-right-join.sql

```
# Use the "my_database" database.
USE my_database ;

# Create a table called "products" with 3 records.
CREATE TABLE IF NOT EXISTS products
( id INT PRIMARY KEY , name CHAR( 20 ) NOT NULL ) ;
INSERT INTO products ( id , name ) VALUES ( 111 , "Socket" ) ;
INSERT INTO products ( id , name ) VALUES ( 222 , "Widget" ) ;
INSERT INTO products ( id , name ) VALUES ( 333 , "Sprocket" ) ;

# Create a table called "orders" with 3 records.
CREATE TABLE IF NOT EXISTS orders
(
  num        INT                 PRIMARY KEY ,
  product    INT ,
  qty        INT ,
  client     CHAR( 20 )
) ;

INSERT INTO orders ( num , product , qty , client )
  VALUES ( 3570 , 222 , 1000 , "Archie" ) ;
```

```
INSERT INTO orders ( num , client )
  VALUES ( 5223 , "Bernie" ) ;
INSERT INTO orders ( num , product , qty , client )
  VALUES ( 4364 , 111 , 800 , "Connie" ) ;
```

```
# Display all products - including those with no orders.
SELECT          p.name AS Product ,
                o.num   AS OrderNumber ,
                o.qty    AS Quantity ,
                o.client AS Client
FROM            products AS p LEFT JOIN orders AS o
ON              p.id = o.product ORDER BY p.name ;
```

```
# Display all orders - including those with no products.
SELECT          o.num   AS OrderNumber ,
                p.name AS Product ,
                o.qty    AS Quantity ,
                o.client AS Client
FROM            products AS p RIGHT JOIN orders AS o
ON              p.id = o.product ORDER BY o.num ;
```

```
# Delete these sample tables.
DROP TABLE IF EXISTS products ;
DROP TABLE IF EXISTS orders ;
```

You may also see these directional joins created using **LEFT OUTER JOIN** and **RIGHT OUTER JOIN** keywords, but in each case the **OUTER** keyword is optional.

When a join is used in a **SELECT** statement always include a join condition – for any type of join.

173

```
CMD MySQL Command Line Client                        —    □    ×

mysql> SOURCE C:\SQL\left-right-join.sql
Database changed

+-----------+-------------+----------+--------+
| Product   | OrderNumber | Quantity | Client |
+-----------+-------------+----------+--------+
| Socket    |        4364 |      800 | Connie |
| Sprocket  |        NULL |     NULL | NULL   |
| Widget    |        3570 |     1000 | Archie |
+-----------+-------------+----------+--------+
3 rows in set (0.00 sec)

+-------------+---------+----------+--------+
| OrderNumber | Product | Quantity | Client |
+-------------+---------+----------+--------+
|        3570 | Widget  |     1000 | Archie |
|        4364 | Socket  |      800 | Connie |
|        5223 | NULL    |     NULL | Bernie |
+-------------+---------+----------+--------+
3 rows in set (0.00 sec)

mysql> _
```

Summary

- A join creates associations between multiple tables within a single **SELECT** statement using the **JOIN** keyword.

- One **SELECT** query can return data from multiple tables by dynamically joining those tables.

- It is more efficient to store duplicating data items in a separate table, then define its relationship to another table by identity.

- The efficient storage of data in numerous related tables is the essence of good relational database design.

- Relational database tables preclude the need to repeatedly input the same data – and they occupy less space too.

- Data stored in a relational database table can be updated by changing just a single record.

- Storing data as a single record in a relational table assures its consistency.

- The name of tables to join are specified as a comma-separated list in a **FROM** clause within a **SELECT** statement.

- Whenever a join is required, a join condition must be specified to define the relationship between the two tables.

- Where multiple tables are joined, multiple join conditions should define their relationships.

- A self join enables a **SELECT** query to make more than one reference to the same table.

- Outer joins can return rows that have no matching relationship.

- **LEFT JOIN** includes all rows in the table specified to the left of the statement, and **RIGHT JOIN** includes all rows from the table to its right.

- The join condition for an inner join is usually specified in a **WHERE** clause, whereas the join condition for an outer join appears after the **ON** keyword instead.

Handy reference

This section contains a description of frequently used SQL statements and typical SQL keywords.

SQL statements

The following pages list some of the most frequently used SQL statements, together with a brief description of their purpose and explanation of their required syntax. Also, the page number is given where the statement is first introduced in this book.

ALTER TABLE
Updates an existing table – precedes one or more alteration statements using the ADD, DROP, or CHANGE keywords [see page 44]

ALTER TABLE *table-name*
  ADD COLUMN *column-name data-type modifiers* ,
  ADD PRIMARY KEY (*column-name*) ,
  DROP COLUMN *column-name* ,
  CHANGE *old-column-name new-column-name*
       data-type modifiers ;

CREATE DATABASE
Creates a new database – can be qualified with
IF NOT EXISTS to check if a database of the specified name already exists [see page 24]

CREATE DATABASE IF NOT EXISTS *database-name* ;

CREATE TABLE
Creates a new database table – precedes parentheses specifying name, data type and optional modifiers for each column. It can be qualified with IF NOT EXISTS to check if a table of the specified name already exists [see page 34]

CREATE TABLE IF NOT EXISTS *table-name*
  (*column-name data-type modifiers* ,
    column-name data-type modifiers) ;

DELETE FROM
Permanently deletes one or more rows from a table –
requires a WHERE clause to identify the row/s to delete. It
will delete all rows without warning if a WHERE clause is
omitted [see page 58]

DELETE FROM *table-name* ;
DELETE FROM *table-name* WHERE *column* = *value* ;

DROP DATABASE
Permanently deletes an existing database – can be qualified
with IF EXISTS to check that a database of the specified
name does indeed exist [see page 26]

DROP DATABASE IF EXISTS *database-name* ;

DROP TABLE
Permanently deletes an existing database table – can
be qualified with IF EXISTS to check that a table of the
specified name does indeed exist [see page 36]

DROP TABLE *table-name* ;
DROP TABLE IF EXISTS *table-name* ;

EXPLAIN
Reveals the format of the specified table, listing column
names, data types and optional modifiers [see page 33]

EXPLAIN *table-name* ;

...SQL statements cont'd

GRANT
Grant statements can create a new user and assign various levels of access privileges. A user's level of privileges can be examined with a SHOW GRANTS statement [see page 130]

GRANT ALL PRIVILEGES ON *.* TO '*user*'@'*domain*' IDENTIFIED BY '*password*' ;

SHOW GRANTS FOR *user@domain* ;

INSERT INTO
Inserts a record into an existing table – precedes the VALUES keyword followed by parentheses containing a comma-separated list of data values. These must match the number of columns and be of appropriate data types [see page 48]

INSERT INTO *table-name* VALUES (*value* , *value* , *value*) ;

A recommended option allows a column list to specify where data should be inserted [see page 50]

INSERT INTO *table-name* (*column* , *column* , *column*) VALUES (*value* , *value* , *value*) ;

Data can be copied from one table into another by replacing the VALUES list with a SELECT statement – the data types must be appropriate in each column [see page 52]

INSERT INTO *destination-table-name*
                (*column* , *column* , *column*)
                    SELECT * FROM *source-table-name* ;

SELECT FROM
Retrieves specified data from an existing database table.
The * wildcard character returns the entire data stored
there or data can be returned for one or more columns by
stating their names as a comma-separated list [see page 62]

SELECT * FROM *table-name* ;
SELECT *column-name* FROM *table-name* ;
SELECT *column , column , column* FROM *table-name* ;

A WHERE clause can be added to a SELECT statement to
identify a particular row or rows [see page 66]

SELECT * FROM *table-name* WHERE *column = value* ;

An ORDER BY clause can be added to the end of a SELECT
statement to determine the alphabetic or numeric order in
which the data returned by the query is sorted
[see page 74]

SELECT * FROM *table-name* ORDER BY *column-name* ;

Data sort order can be explicitly set as ascending or
descending by adding the ASC or DESC keyword at the end
of an ORDER BY clause – if not specified, ascending order is
assumed [see page 80]

SELECT * FROM *table-name*
  ORDER BY *column-name* DESC ;

A WHERE clause can compare data in multiple columns
with the OR and AND logical operators [see page 96]

SELECT * FROM *table-name*
  WHERE *column-name = value*
  AND *column-name = value* ;

SELECT FROM (continued)

Column data can be compared against multiple inclusive alternatives with the IN keyword – this precedes parentheses containing the comma-separated list of alternative values.
Similarly, multiple exclusive values can be compared with the NOT IN keywords [see page 100]

SELECT * FROM *table-name*
  WHERE *column-name* IN (*value* , *value* , *value*)
  AND *column-name* NOT IN (*value* , *value* , *value*) ;

Textual column data can be compared against a search pattern using the LIKE keyword – the query will return all matches that are similar to the specified pattern [see page 104]

SELECT * FROM *table-name*
  WHERE *column-name* LIKE *search-pattern* ;

Alias names can be specified for columns with the AS keyword [see page 116]

SELECT *column-name-1* AS *col1* ,
        column-name-2 AS *col2*
        FROM *table-name* ;

Data returned by a SELECT query can be grouped around the column specified in a GROUP BY clause [see page 142]

SELECT * FROM *table-name*
GROUP BY *column-name* ;

Grouped data can be filtered with a HAVING clause – row data is filtered by the WHERE clause [see page 144]

SELECT * FROM *table-name*
GROUP BY *column-name* HAVING *expression* ;

SELECT FROM (continued)

Data can be selected from one or more joined tables using the JOIN keyword [see page 164]

SELECT * FROM *table-name* JOIN *table-name* ;

SHOW DATABASES
Lists the names of all databases in the DBMS [see page 23]

SHOW DATABASES ;

SHOW TABLES
Lists the names of all tables within the currently selected database [see page 32]

SHOW TABLES ;

UPDATE
Replaces data in one or more columns of a table – precedes a SET statement specifying one or more columns and values. It requires a WHERE clause to identify the row/s to update otherwise it will update all rows without warning [see page 56]

UPDATE *table-name* SET *column-name* = *value* ;
UPDATE *table-name*
   SET *column-name* = *value* , *column-name* = *value*
   WHERE *column* = *value* ;

USE
Selects a database in which to add, manipulate or retrieve table data [see page 32]

USE *database-name* ;

SQL keywords

The following tables in the remainder of this appendix list keywords that have special meaning in SQL. These are known as "reserved" words and should not be used when naming databases, tables, columns or any other objects within a SQL database – using a keyword in a name will generate an error.

DBMSs tend to support a specific set of keywords so not all the keywords listed in these tables are supported by any one DBMS – the listed keywords are reserved in MySQL 8 for example.

In addition to the keywords listed in the following tables, some DBMSs have further extended this list of SQL reserved words with their own implementation-specific keywords. The documentation for each DBMS will normally list all the keywords that it supports.

Except for their intended purpose, it is strongly recommended that the use of all reserved words should be avoided – even those which are not currently supported by your own DBMS. This should ensure that the SQL code remains portable and compatible with new releases of all DBMSs.

ACCESSIBLE	ADD	ALL
ALTER	ANALYZE	AND
AS	ASC	ASENSITIVE
BEFORE	BETWEEN	BIGINT
BINARY	BLOB	BOTH
BY	CALL	CASCADE
CASE	CHANGE	CHAR
CHARACTER	CHECK	COLLATE
COLUMN	CONDITION	CONSTRAINT
CONTINUE	CONVERT	CREATE

CROSS	CUBE	CURRENT_DATE
CURRENT_TIME	CURRENT_TIMESTAMP	CURRENT_USER
CURSOR	DATABASE	DATABASES
DAY_HOUR	DAY_MICROSECOND	DAY_MINUTE
DAY_SECOND	DEC	DECIMAL
DECLARE	DEFAULT	DELAYED
DELETE	DENSE_RANK	DESC
DESCRIBE	DETERMINISTIC	DISTINCT
DISTINCTION	DIV	DOUBLE
DROP	DUAL	EACH
ELSE	ELSEIF	EMPTY
ENCLOSED	ESCAPED	EXCEPT
EXISTS	EXIT	EXPLAIN
FALSE	FETCH	FIRST_VALUE
FLOAT	FLOAT4	FLOAT8
FOR	FORCE	FOREIGN
FROM	FULLTEXT	FUNCTION
GENERATED	GET	GRANT
GROUP	GROUPING	GROUPS
HAVING	HIGH_PRIORITY	HOUR_MICROSECOND

...SQL keywords cont'd

HOUR_MINUTE	HOUR_SECOND	IF
IGNORE	IN	INDEX
INFILE	INNER	INOUT
INSENSITIVE	INSERT	INT
INT1	INT2	INT3
INT4	INT8	INTEGER
INTERVAL	INTO	IO_AFTER_GTIDS
IO_BEFORE_GTIDS	IS	ITERATE
JOIN	JSON_TABLE	KEY
KEYS	KILL	LAG
LAST_VALUE	LATERAL	LEAD
LEADING	LEAVE	LEFT
LIKE	LIMIT	LINEAR
LINES	LOAD	LOCALTIME
LOCALTIMESTAMP	LOCK	LONG
LONGBLOB	LONGTEXT	LOOP
LOW_PRIORITY	MASTER_BIND	MASTER_SSL_VERIFY_SERVER_CERT
MATCH	MAXVALUE	MEDIUMBLOB
MEDIUMINT	MEDIUMTEXT	MIDDLEINT
MINUTE_MICROSECOND	MINUTE_SECOND	MOD

MODIFIES	NATURAL	NOT
NO_WRITE_TO_BINLOG	NTH_VALUE	NTILE
NULL	NUMERIC	OF
OLD	ON	OPTIMIZE
OPTIMIZER_COSTS	OPTION	OPTIONALLY
OR	ORDER	OUT
OUTER	OUTFILE	OVER
PARTITION	PERCENT_RANK	PRECISION
PRIMARY	PROCEDURE	PURGE
RANGE	RANK	READ
READS	READ_WRITE	REAL
RECURSIVE	REFERENCES	REGEXP
RELEASE	RENAME	REPEAT
REPLACE	REQUIRE	RESIGNAL
RESTRICT	RETURN	REVOKE
RIGHT	RLIKE	ROW
ROWS	ROW_NUMBER	SCHEMA
SCHEMAS	SECOND_MICROSECOND	SELECT
SENSITIVE	SEPARATOR	SET
SHOW	SIGNAL	SMALLINT

…SQL keywords cont'd

SPATIAL	SPECIFIC	SQL
SQLEXCEPTION	SQLSTATE	SQLWARNING
SQL_BIG_RESULT	SQL_CALC_FOUND_ROWS	SQL_SMALL_RESULT
SSL	STARTING	STORED
STRAIGHT_JOIN	SYSTEM	TABLE
TERMINATED	THEN	TINYBLOB
TINYINT	TINYTEXT	TO
TRAILING	TRIGGER	TRUE
UNDO	UNION	UNIQUE
UNLOCK	UNSIGNED	UPDATE
USAGE	USE	USING
UTC_DATE	UTC_TIME	UTC_TIMESTAMP
VALUES	VARBINARY	VARCHAR
VARCHARACTER	VARYING	VIRTUAL
WHEN	WHERE	WHILE
WINDOW	WITH	WRITE
XOR	YEAR_MONTH	ZEROFILL

H

I

J

K

L

N

M

O

T

U

V

W

Y